Dermot Bolger was born in Dublin in 1959. He is the author of four novels: *Night Shift*, which received the AE Memorial Award, the controversial, bestselling *The Journey Home* (Penguin 1991), which was shortlisted for the *Irish Times*/Aer Lingus Irish Literature Award, *The Woman's Daughter* (Penguin 1992), which received the Macaulay Fellowship, and *Emily's Shoes* (Viking 1992). His first play, *The Lament for Arthur Cleary*, one of the major hits of the 1989 Dublin Theatre Festival and the 1990 Edinburgh Festival, received the Stewart Parker BBC Award, an Edinburgh Fringe First, the 1990 Samuel Beckett Award for the best first play seen in Britain, and has been broadcast on BBC Radio 4. The author of five volumes of poetry, Dermot Bolger is editor of the Raven Arts Press, one of Ireland's most radical publishers, and is a member of The Arts Council of Ireland.

DERMOT BOLGER

A DUBLIN QUARTET

WITH AN INTRODUCTION BY FINTAN O'TOOLE

PENGUIN BOOKS

PENGUIN BOOKS

Published by the Penguin Group
Penguin Books Ltd, 27 Wrights Lane, London w8 5TZ, England
Penguin Books USA Inc., 375 Hudson Street, New York, New York 10014, USA
Penguin Books Australia Ltd, Ringwood, Victoria, Australia
Penguin Books Canada Ltd, 10 Alcorn Avenue, Toronto, Ontario, Canada M4V 3B2
Penguin Books (NZ) Ltd, 182–190 Wairau Road, Auckland 10, New Zealand

Penguin Books Ltd, Registered Offices: Harmondsworth, Middlesex, England

An early version of *The Lament for Arthur Cleary* was first published by
Nick Hern Books, a division of Walker Books Ltd,
in an anthology entitled *The Crack in the Emerald*, 1990
This collection first published 1992
1 3 5 7 9 10 8 6 4 2

Copyright © Dermot Bolger, 1990, 1992
Introduction copyright © Fintan O'Toole, 1992
All rights reserved

The moral right of the author has been asserted

All rights whatsoever in these plays are strictly reserved,
and application for performance should be made, before rehearsal,
to A. P. Watt Ltd, 20 John Street, London WC1N 2DR

Printed in England by Clays Ltd, St Ives plc
Filmset in Monophoto Plantin Light

Except in the United States of America, this book is sold subject
to the condition that it shall not, by way of trade or otherwise, be lent,
re-sold, hired out, or otherwise circulated without the publisher's
prior consent in any form of binding or cover other than that in
which it is published and without a similar condition including this
condition being imposed on the subsequent purchaser

For David Byrne, with thanks

CONTENTS

AUTHOR'S NOTE

When one of America's finest songwriters was once asked 'What came first, the music or the lyrics?' he replied 'The phone call.' Although the product of many things, the plays in this book have firstly all been the result of phone calls. To the people who had the faith in me to make those calls, especially Niall O'Baoill and David Byrne of Wet Paint who (at the same time as Vincent Dowling of The Abbey Theatre commissioned my play *Blinded by the Light* – a comedy which is not part of this quartet) asked me for a play at a time when I had no theatrical experience or background, I owe a great deal of thanks – as I do, for later calls, to Michael Colgan of the Gate Theatre and Garry Hynes of The Abbey.

The première of *One Last White Horse* in the Dublin Theatre Festival in the autumn of 1991 was my fifth opening night in twenty-five months. Few new writers can have been so privileged as to learn their craft by working on some of the finest stages in Ireland and with the cream of Irish acting talent. From each of them I have learned something and to each I give thanks: Owen Roe, Brendan Laird, Berts Folan, Hilary Fannin and Lynn Cahill, and especially Maureen White (a wonderful dramaturge) in the original production of *Arthur Cleary* in Dublin, Edinburgh and London; Liam Cummingham and Eamonn Hunt who played in the Irish tour and in America; Brendan Gleeson (who played Arthur) and many others in the BBC Radio production; Donal O'Kelly and Alison Deegan (two *tour de force* performances) along with Gerard Byrne, Phelim Drew, Kevin Flood, Michael James

Ford, Frank Kelly, Wesley Murphy, Maire Ni Ghrainne, Enda Oates and Maurie Taylor – and especially director Caroline Fitzgerald in *Blinded by the Light* and the brave solo playing of Stephen Brennan and Pat Leavy in *The Tramway End*. And to many of the same actors again, along with Des Braidan, Barbara Brennan, Bernie Downes, Peadar Lamb and Macdara Ó Fátharta in *One Last White Horse*. But more especially, although this is a book of plays by Dermot Bolger, it is also very much a set of four plays directed by David Byrne. To no other person do I owe a greater debt as a playwright.

A special final word of praise is due to Wet Paint in Dublin who in recent years have quietly built up a network of community venues where they tour new and highly innovative professional theatre to an audience which has never experienced theatre before.

After its run in the Dublin Theatre Festival, *The Lament for Arthur Cleary* began its touring life playing on makeshift stages in small community halls in the suburbs of Dublin city and county. The set was fitted up anywhere it would go, as backstage people like Ned McLoughlin and Sinead Connolly fought seemingly impossible battles to get each production mounted. If Festival audiences were quiet during the opening blackouts, here they could shout and mock. Often at times the cast faced hostility yet every night, through their intense commitment and talent, one could hear a pin drop by the start of the second act as the cast won.

I have seen the play in many different cities since, and yet no matter where it opens when the lights go down for the opening blackout I still see those makeshift venues in the Dublin suburbs on winter's evenings, feel the same fear in my throat, and the same tingle of excitement that is the unique magic of theatre. May the other plays here have as interesting lives.

Dermot Bolger
Dublin, 1991

x

ON THE FRONTIER

by Fintan O'Toole

Dublin is now a frontier town, on the edge of Europe, on the edge of the Irish nation, on the edge of itself. The city now exists largely at its own extremes. In the last thirty years it has ceased to be the teeming, intense and intimate city that Joyce and O'Casey made use of and become a sprawling place, stretching its limbs over old villages, over farmland, up the sides of the hills. As the old inner city – the city whose ironies of classical architecture inhabited by class-ridden poverty created the bitter humour of its people – has become gap-toothed with dereliction, so the new suburbs have been voraciously eating up the surrounding countryside. New places have been born, places without history, without the accumulated resonances of centuries, places that prefigure the end of the fierce notion of Irishness that sustained the state for seventy years. Sex and drugs and rock 'n' roll are more important in the new places than the old Irish totems of Land, Nationality and Catholicism. Dermot Bolger comes from one of these places, the working-class suburb of Finglas to the north of the city, and his work is marked by this fact.

The loss of a sense of history is also a liberation from the shackles of the past. Joyce's Stephen Dedalus regarded history as a nightmare from which he was trying to awake, but in the suburbs that nightmare is buried beneath concrete and tarmac. The juggernauts whizzing by on the motorway carry not the burden of history but goods for export from the Most Profitable Location in Europe for American Industry, as the ads in *Time* magazine call the new Ireland. The great tradition of

Irish writing is silent on the subject of suburbs, so you can slip out from under its shadow. No one has ever mythologized this housing estate, this footbridge over the motorway, that video rental shop. It is, for the writer, virgin territory.

A loss, though, is still a loss. We need to shape our lives with some sense of significance, some notion of a journey that ties together past, present and future. If history is not given to us, we need to invent it, to create personal histories, to map out private journeys. This is not the sense of loss that creates nostalgia, of which there is hardly a trace in Dermot Bolger's plays, but the sense of loss that creates a hole that must be filled. The liberation from the past is physically present in these plays, in their formal adventurousness, their deeply European character, the search in their language for a poetry of the unpoetic, the everyday. But if the liberation creates the framework for these plays, the loss creates the hunger that drives their characters. Their restlessness, their need to undertake voyages, their search for a vaguely discerned home, all come from a feeling that something has been misplaced and cannot be found again. In these plays you can go back but you can never return; you can seek but you can never find.

If you see yourself as being in a tradition, as part of a historic story that is still playing itself out, then you are not free to step outside that story, rewrite bits of the plot, remember the language of the early scenes, invent new endings. Belonging to no obvious tradition, either in a literary sense or in the wider sense of being part of a traditional Ireland, Dermot Bolger is free to do precisely these things, and that freedom helps to shape these plays. Two apparently fixed and sacred aspects of the Irish tradition are the Gaelic language, with its languid and sorrowful literature, and Catholicism. Both seem very far in time and place from the world of Dermot Bolger's plays, yet precisely because of that distance both are available to him to shape in his own way, to bend to the inflections of his own accent.

The Lament for Arthur Cleary is inspired by one of the most famous poems in the Gaelic language, 'Caoineadh Airt Ui

Laoire', a lament for a man who dies because he cannot bend his pride to the demands of oppressive English rule, cannot understand that the Ireland he left to go and fight on the Continent has, on his return, become a more dangerous place. *The Holy Ground*, less obviously, draws on a great Gaelic love poem in which the writer complains that his love has stolen God away from him. But in both cases the Gaelic sources are used not to place the plays in an unbroken tradition but to suggest parallels between Ireland now, fractured and confused as it is, and the broken, dissolving, powerfully angry world of the last days of a dying Gaelic civilization. It is not an unbroken tradition but a tradition of *being broken* that is at issue. If there is a history at work, it is a history of one world giving way painfully to another, just as in the suburbs of Dublin one world is giving way to another one, more uncertain but less confined.

The sense of things dead or dying is everywhere in the plays. In *The Lament for Arthur Cleary* the central character is already dead, and the play itself is enacted on the borders of death and life. *One Last White Horse* takes place in the mind of a dying man, shoots through the memory cells of a brain full of heroin. Heroin, the death-bringer, the suburban Nemesis of our times, is a principal actor in both of these plays, an image both of a dying Dublin and of the radical openness of the new city, willing to embrace anything that is going, innocent and raw and wild and vulnerable enough in the early 1980s to become, for a time, the heroin capital of Europe. And, in less dramatic ways, other deaths – the death of a husband, the death of a father – hang over the two shorter plays in this volume.

This concentration on death, though, should also alert us to the spiritual quest that is being undertaken in these plays. The second element of the Irish past that emerges here is Catholicism, and it is revived in strange ways. Bolger's plays have been rightly praised for their realism, for the way in which they reflect, and reflect on, a changed set of social circumstances. But it must be remembered that Irish reality itself

3

remains deeply imbued with an often surreal religiosity. There is again a paradox: one of the ways you knew that traditional Ireland was breaking down in the last few years was the resurgence of a despairing, bitter Catholicism, manifested in everything from the insertion of a clause into the Irish Constitution prohibiting abortion to the defeat of an attempt to permit divorce and to the crowds who gathered in fields or churchyards on summer evenings to watch statues of the Blessed Virgin waving, dancing and weeping. This too was social reality, however surreal, and Dermot Bolger has not been afraid to engage with it in his work.

The world of Dermot Bolger's plays is godless, but it is not irreligious. The complaint of a woman who has just buried her husband that the dead man, with his almost psychotic fanaticism, stole her Christ from her is the key to this world from which God is absent, but the need, the search, for some other God cannot be avoided. The terraces of German football stadiums during the European Championship become the site for a sort of Mass at which the congregation of the Irish diaspora offers the only prayer to the vanished God that it can muster: the chant 'IRELAND, IRELAND, IRELAND'. The border guards who bar the way on Arthur Cleary's voyage are also angels guarding the gates of Heaven or Hell. The 'last white horse' is heroin, or the ghost of Eddie's mother, or the Blessed Virgin, and Eddie's pursuit of the drug is a desperate attempt to fill a hole that has been left by the banishment of childhood religious belief.

Because Irish reality has become increasingly surreal, the usual division in writing between the realist on the one hand and the fantasist on the other has begun to break down. Realism has to become surrealism; naturalism has to become supernaturalism. Dermot Bolger's work is at the forefront of this development. On the one hand, he deals with areas of Irish reality that have largely been avoided by the theatre heretofore: modern urban life, the new, shifting, unsentimental emigration, the plague of heroin, the realities of poverty at the uneasy edge of the European Community. He is, in that sense, a realistic writer, counterposing a new grasp of what it is like to live in urban Ireland now to the old pieties of place and character and landscape. On the other hand, though, his realism is not naturalistic. These plays are not descriptions of a world; they are forays into it. They reflect the world they inhabit just as the steamed-up window of a bus reflects the face of a child drawing pictures on it, an image that is used in *One Last White Horse*. The face is real; the setting is resolutely downbeat; but the image that is reflected has its own surreal logic, and the pictures that are drawn on it are the cyphers of the imagination.

The weakness of much of social realism in the theatre has always been its refusal to accept that dreams, fantasies, the products of the imagination are not escapes from everyday reality but integral parts of that reality. Ireland itself is the product of dreams – the dreams of Independence first, then the dreams of modernity, the American dreams of high-tech foreigners coming to make all the failures right. And in these plays the dreams come in waves: the political dreams, the dream-worlds of soccer and television, the dreams of family, of recapturing a lost time, the imagined children who animate Monica's life in *The Holy Ground*. Both of the full-length plays have this overwhelmingly dream-like quality without ever giving way to the obscurity and self-indulgence that dreams can be a licence for.

Ireland, it should be remembered, is a country described by its own Taoiseach (Prime Minister) as 'a dream which has yet to be fulfilled'. When a real place is seen even by those who run it as a dream, then real people are left with dreams, aspirations, fantasies to live on. In *One Last White Horse* Eddie's unbearable Ireland shrinks to a pulse inside his own head. Arthur Cleary's Ireland is ground that has shifted, already a place of the memory. Eoin's Ireland is a temporary vision conjured up on the terraces of a foreign stadium by eleven men in green jerseys, a vision as evanescent as any moving statue. Monica's Ireland is a picture of another woman's child sent in a letter home from a foreign country.

These are stateless persons, undocumented aliens in their own country, unable to know their place because their place has become unknowable. They are the state of a nation.

But they are more than that, too. The very restlessness, the shifting, open, unformed nature of the world of these plays, makes them also European. Here we have not just an unofficial Ireland but also an unofficial Europe, the Europe of the *Gastarbeiter* and the long-haul truck driver, the Europe of the football hooligan and the border guard. The people of these plays abolished the borders long ago, driven to do so by both economic and spiritual needs. In the common European house they squat in the lower storeys. Unlike the more settled residents, they are forced to live in Europe, to cross its borders and follow its shifts, to negotiate it rather than merely to occupy a fixed place within it. If they belong anywhere, these plays belong to the Europe that is now stretching itself untidily from Connemara to the Caucasus, trying to find a comfortable place to lay its increasingly uneasy head.

THE LAMENT
FOR ARTHUR CLEARY

'*The Lament for Arthur Cleary* is a joyous celebration of the old strumpet city itself, a love-poem to the city of Dublin, to its people, its streets, its housing estates, but above all to that indomitable Dublin spirit.

Sunday Tribune

'If the 30th Dublin Theatre Festival achieves nothing more, it could well be remembered as the launch pad for Dermot Bolger's first play, *The Lament for Arthur Cleary*.'

Sunday Independent

'You won't see a better first Irish play this year than Dermot Bolger's *The Lament for Arthur Cleary*.'

Guardian

CHARACTERS

ARTHUR CLEARY, a Dubliner in his mid-thirties

GIRL, his girlfriend who goes to live with him

FRONTIER GUARD

PORTER

FRIEND (a woman)

all of whom play a variety
of interchanging roles

The Lament for Arthur Cleary was first performed by
Wet Paint Arts as part of the Dublin Theatre Festival
at the Project Arts Centre on 18 September 1989. The
cast was as follows:

ARTHUR CLEARY	Brendan Laird
GIRL	Hilary Fannin
FRONTIER GUARD	Owen Roe
PORTER	Berts Folan
FRIEND	Lynn Cahill
Director	David Byrne
Dramaturg	Maureen White
Stage Director	Sinead Connolly
Designer	Ned McLoughlin
Music by	Gerard Grennell
Costumes by	Maire Tierney

ACT ONE

As the first strains of music begin, the actors file slowly out on to the stage. The FRIEND, *the* FRONTIER GUARD *and the* PORTER *in that order stand at the back of the stage with sticks in their hands.* ARTHUR CLEARY *goes to sit on a small box in the front right-hand corner and the* GIRL *takes centre-stage. There is a raised wooden platform (about six feet high and two feet across) in the centre of the stage and a barrel at the far right where the* FRIEND *is standing. When the* GIRL *begins to recite, her voice is echoed by a recording of itself over the music which grows in tempo.*

GIRL: My lament for you Arthur Cleary
           As you lay down that crooked back lane
              Under the stern wall of a factory
           Where moss and crippled flowers cling.

              I cupped your face in my palms
           To taste life draining from your lips
              And you died attempting to smile
           As defiant and proud as you had lived.

(The stage goes black and across the music comes the sharp banging of sticks on both the barrel and the wooden supports of the backdrop. They grow in fury until they are almost drowned by the scream of pipes in the soundtrack. There is sudden silence. In the growing dim light we can discern the three figures who are each holding a death mask over their

faces and standing poised with sticks raised. After they have each spoken once they will slowly converge on ARTHUR *sitting on the box and the* GIRL *who is sleeping uneasily, twisting in dreams under a white cloth at his feet. Each sentence is accompanied by a sharp thud of a stick.*)

PORTER: (*Resigned*) It's dead Arthur, don't you know it's dead?

FRIEND: (*Defiant*) When did we ever care about them, son? When did we ever?

FRONTIER GUARD: (*Menacingly*) Decide Cleary. With me or against me.

FRIEND: (*Spiteful*) You'd go off with him, that old cripple.

(*She slaps her stick against the barrel beside her on the last word. They move forward, chanting phrases from their sentences which are slightly jumbled into each other but sufficiently spaced to be distinctive. There are a number of sharp bangs of sticks as they approach, which unnerve* ARTHUR. *The* PORTER *laughs mockingly in a low tone. They gather behind* ARTHUR *and with one final thud, this time on the box he is sitting on, they raise their sticks in a fan behind his back. At this final thud the* GIRL *jerks awake and sits bolt upright, her back against* ARTHUR, *the sheet clutched protectively against her.* ARTHUR *reaches down, soothing her.*)

ARTHUR: Bad dream, love, just a bad dream.

(*The* GIRL *looks at him as though coming back to her senses and then stares forward.*)

GIRL: I'm frightened, Arthur. I dreamt it again.

ARTHUR: The same one? Can you remember it?

(*She tries to think and shakes her head.*)

GIRL: No, but it was the same one. It's always gone when I wake but I know it. I know the fear in it. Like the fear of nothing else. (*Pause.*) Let's go Arthur, now, while we've still time.

ARTHUR: (*Half amused/half soothing*) Go away? Listen, love, I've finally come home. This is our home. Nobody can take it from us. Home. Say it.

GIRL: (*Nervously*) Home?

ARTHUR: (*Firmly*) Home.

GIRL: (*Less tentatively*) Home.

ARTHUR: (*Firmly*) Home.

(*His arm nestling her head, they lie back slowly as they repeat the word. The lights go down into blackness.*)

ARTHUR *and* GIRL: (*Firmly*) Home.

(*A new music begins, eerie, unsettling with the hint of the noise of trains. A spotlight switches on, held by the* FRONTIER GUARD. *It flickers over the stage.*)

FRONTIER GUARD: Check the wheels!

PORTER: For what?

FRONTIER GUARD: (*Dismissively*) Just do it!

(*From behind the raised platform the* PORTER *switches on his torch. Its beam moves up and down the wooden bars in front of which* ARTHUR *stands in semi-darkness with a green passport in his hand. The* FRONTIER GUARD *enters behind him.*)
Passport, please.

(ARTHUR *turns.*)

ARTHUR: Oh, sorry.

(*He hands him his passport which the* FRONTIER GUARD *opens and examines.*)

FRONTIER GUARD: Ah Irish. Boom-boom! Eh!

(*He laughs.*)

ARTHUR: Yeah. Boom-bleeding-boom.

(*The* FRONTIER GUARD *hands him back his passport.*)

FRONTIER GUARD *and* PORTER: (*Ironically as they circle with torches*)

> We are green, we are white,
> We are Irish dynamite!

ARTHUR: Eh, do you mind me asking? Where am I now? Which side of the border am I on?

FRONTIER GUARD: (*Stops and shrugs his shoulders*) What difference to you, Irish? I see you people every day, you're going this way, you're going that way, but never home. Either way you're a long way from there.

ARTHUR: (*Nods his head towards the window*) What's he looking at the wheels for?

FRONTIER GUARD: Looking for? It is the rules, Irish. He does what he is told. If you ordered him to look for a snowball in a fire he would sit staring all night.

(FRONTIER GUARD *laughs as he stares out at the* PORTER *walking with the torch, then turns abruptly, snapping back into his official voice.*)

We will go on soon.

(*He exits as the* PORTER *comes around to* ARTHUR's *side of the platform, still shining the torch up and down.*)

ARTHUR: What difference does it make? (*He looks up and down.*) Another limbo of tracks and warehouses. Could be anywhere. (*He gives a half laugh.*) Except home.

PORTER: (*Looking up and shining torch directly at his face*) How can you leave a place when you're carrying it round inside you, Cleary? And after a time you can only go there in your mind. Because when you go back you can feel . . . the distance, eh. The big town just a squalid village, the big man . . . what's that you call him . . . a crock of shit. You say nothing, but you know and . . . wait till you see, Cleary . . . the big men, the bosses, they know you know.

ARTHUR: (*Moving to window and staring down at him in astonishment*) How do you know my name? I don't know you.

PORTER: You don't know nothing.

(*He switches torch off and scurries forward to set up the wooden box on the front left of the stage. The* FRIEND *comes striding forward in confident pose towards the box. The other four characters have gathered together in front of the raised platform and have begun clapping as soon as the torch is switched off. The* FRIEND *clears her throat and then silences the others with a grand sweep of her hand. She stares in front of her. There is applause scattered throughout her speech, which she halts by the use of her hand.*)

FRIEND: (*In smooth politician's voice*) Although we are a small nation in this great community, our heritage abounds with saints, with poets, with dreamers. Though we in government are realists, first and foremost. We know we cannot all live in this one island. But we are not ashamed. Young

people are to Ireland what champagne is to France! Our
finest crop, the cream of our youth, nurtured from birth,
raised with tender love by our young state, brought to
ripeness and then plucked! For export to your factories
and offices. Fellow European ministers, we are but a
small land with a small role to play in this great union of
nations. But a land with a great history. Long before
Columbus set sail in 1492, long before Amerigo Vespucci
gave his name to that great continent – (*Applause takes
on rhythmic effect.*) – our missionaries in their boats of
animal hide had already discovered the new world.
Through all of the dark ages we have fought to spread the
word of God among you – (*Others bless themselves.*) – to
petition you for arms to repel our invader – (*Others join
hands and grimace.*) – to fight your wars. Once more we
entrust to you the flower of our youth, not black –

OTHERS: Oh no –
FRIEND: Or yellow –
OTHERS: Oh no –
FRIEND: But white –
OTHERS: Oh yes –
FRIEND: Not illiterate –
OTHERS: Oh no –
FRIEND: Or backward –
OTHERS: Oh no –
FRIEND: But qualified –
OTHERS: Oh yes –
FRIEND: Not migrants –
OTHERS: Oh no –
FRIEND: Or illegals –
OTHERS: Oh no –
FRIEND: But as equal Europeans.
(*Great applause from the others.*)

We know they are ready to take their place, we know you
will not turn your back on them. (*Slight pause.*) And now
my fellow minister will give a brief discourse on night-life
in Dublin. Thank you.

(*She steps down and the* PORTER *lifts her round into the centre of the stage where she and the* GIRL *begin to dance to the disco beat which is growing louder. The* PORTER *lifts the box away to one side and then walks slightly drunkenly over to the far side of the stage. The* FRONTIER GUARD *clicks his fingers, checks his suit and stands self-importantly beside the raised platform as lights begin to spin so that the stage becomes awash with speckled light suggesting a night-club. In the corner the two* GIRLS *are seen, checking their make-up, miming a conversation with themselves. The* FRONTIER GUARD *is passive, self-assured. He puts an arm out as though blocking the doorway, well aware of his strength. The* PORTER *backs away and then approaches, nervous, gazing up at the doorway. He stops.* FRONTIER GUARD *ignores him.* PORTER *moves closer.*)

PORTER: What's it like inside, Mister?

(*The* FRONTIER GUARD *unfolds his hands and looks down at him. He speaks slowly as if to a child but also like a seedy Soho doorman.*)

FRONTIER GUARD: Everything you ever dreamt of. Girls hot for it, lining the walls, leather mini-skirts, thighs like long stalks of barley waiting to be harvested.

PORTER: It's that good, is it?

FRONTIER GUARD: It's better.

PORTER: So, eh, I suppose . . . is there . . . eh, any chance . . . ?

FRONTIER GUARD: Ever hear of Matt Talbot's first miracle?

PORTER: Eh, no.

FRONTIER GUARD: Brothers they were, out in Ballybough. Three of them. Dockers. Down the kips in Monto every weekend. All three of them contracted it. (*Pause.*) The pox! Worst dose imaginable. Only one cure you know.

(*He raises two fingers sideways to form a scissors and makes a cut down at the* PORTER's *zip. The* PORTER *jumps back.*)

Matt Talbot was their only hope. He says to them, 'Go down to the Liffey before dawn every morning for a week, strip naked, cover yourselves in muck and beg God for forgiveness.'

(*He pauses.*)

PORTER: And were they cured?

FRONTIER GUARD: (*Tone changing as he advances*) No! And the first miracle of Matt Talbot was that they didn't murder the little runt afterwards. And it would take a second bloody miracle by him to get the likes of you in here. So get the hell away from this door!

(*The* PORTER *retreats as* ARTHUR *approaches.* ARTHUR *watches him back off and looks at the* FRONTIER GUARD *who shrugs his shoulders.*)

Kids! (*Looks at him again.*) Think they own the world after a pint of Harp. You looking for something?

(ARTHUR *looks over the* FRONTIER GUARD's *head, tracing an outline with his hand.*)

ARTHUR: A fish used to be there.

FRONTIER GUARD: (*Looking at him*) So were the Vikings.

ARTHUR: (*Pointing*) No, you can still see the outline of the sign.

FRONTIER GUARD: (*Looking up*) Jaysus you can too. That wasn't today or yesterday.

ARTHUR: The Rock Salmon Club. Used to be my regular. Great bands, poxy name.

FRONTIER GUARD: Yeah, I remember it. That was what . . . God, it's closed over ten years now. Went there a few times myself. Never thought I'd wind up working on the door. I was barred from it often enough. Well, you know yourself.

ARTHUR: Will you stop. I'd me skull busted in here once. They closed the gaff for a while after. What's it now?

FRONTIER GUARD: Bop de bop bop (*moves his hands to make shapes*) around the handbags. Under twelves with adults. Have you been away or what?

ARTHUR: Yeah. For too long I think. Thought this place might be the same.

FRONTIER GUARD: Just kids now, disco beat. You're welcome to have a look.

ARTHUR: Naw, you're all right. Thanks anyway. I'll see you round.

FRONTIER GUARD: Yeah, good luck. (*Looks over* ARTHUR's *shoulder and talks to himself.*) Ah, here we go time, the terrible twins.

(*As* ARTHUR *wanders off the two* GIRLS *have appeared.*)

GIRL: Oh God, it's him. Not here, Sharon. Let's go somewhere else.

FRIEND: Where then?

GIRL: Anywhere. I hate him.

FRIEND: Just to be nice to him only takes a minute and you're in. You rub him up wrong.

GIRL: (*Shudders*) It's him rubbing me up I hate.

FRIEND: So listen, what are our choices, what do you fancy doing? Stand around the streets all night . . .

(*The* PORTER *passes and leers at her. He roars.*)

. . . get a bus home, sit with your Da, take up knitting.

GIRL: (*Imitating knitting movements*) All right, I'll go in. But you first.

FRIEND: (*Warning her*) And you keep your trap shut, do you hear. You get us in enough bloody trouble.

(*They approach the* FRONTIER GUARD.)

FRONTIER GUARD: Well, girls. Anything I can do for you? Suggestions? Requests?

FRIEND: You couldn't try letting us in for a change, Frank?

FRONTIER GUARD: Might have to frisk you first, girls. Need to protect my punters.

FRIEND: You're not the only night-club in this street.

FRONTIER GUARD: The only one that serves under-twelves like you. Does your Da know you're out . . . wearing that? So how about it . . . one kiss?

(*The* PORTER *has joined the queue behind the* GIRL. *The* FRIEND *looks back at him.*)

FRIEND: Your boyfriend might get jealous. Come on, Frank, please, it's cold.

FRONTIER GUARD: You could try wearing clothes . . . those skimpy things, flaunting yourselves. No, I'd have a moral objection.

FRIEND: Come on, Frank, please.

FRONTIER GUARD: The Brownies meeting is over, girls. Past your bedtime.

FRIEND: You know us, Frank, you let us in last week. We even have comps. We got them in the pub.

(*She produces two cards which she hands to him.*)

FRONTIER GUARD: How's your little moody friend tonight? Still stuck up. (*Looks past* FRIEND *at* GIRL *and eyes her.*) So do you call that a dress or an undress?

GIRL: I see why they call them monkey suits.

(FRONTIER GUARD *looks past her at the* PORTER, *who grins.*)

FRONTIER GUARD: What do you want, Chink? No seagulls for your curry in here. Try Dollymount Strand. Go on.

PORTER: Just want to dance, what's it to you?

FRONTIER GUARD: Come up here, and we'll see if you're as yellow as your skin. Back to your own country, boy.

PORTER: I was born here.

FRONTIER GUARD: (*Tone quieter*) Come here a second, sonny, I won't hurt you.

(PORTER *approaches.*)

PORTER: What?

(FRONTIER GUARD *flicks him around and twists his arm behind his back.*)

FRONTIER GUARD: You weren't born anywhere. You were hatched out in the sun.

(*He shoves him and the* PORTER *half stumbles offstage.*) Well, girls . . . ?

GIRL: Bastard.

FRIEND: (*Hissing to* GIRL) Shut up. (*To* FRONTIER GUARD) Frank, come on, we've . . .

FRONTIER GUARD: (*Snaps*) Get out of my sight. Now!

FRIEND: Apologize to Frank.

GIRL: I will not.

(GIRLS *back away arguing to left as* ARTHUR *approaches from right.* FRONTIER GUARD *turns.*)

FRONTIER GUARD: You back again?

ARTHUR: I'll take you up on that offer.

FRONTIER GUARD: What?

ARTHUR: See the gaff . . . memories.

(FRONTIER GUARD *shrugs his shoulders*.)

FRONTIER GUARD: Ah, listen, I'd have second thoughts. You'll get nothing in there except odd looks.

ARTHUR: Not looking for anything.

(*The* GIRLS *have been miming a discussion at back of stage during the last few pieces of conversation*.)

FRONTIER GUARD: I'm not supposed to allow jeans, for a start.

ARTHUR: Old time's sake, mate.

(*The* PORTER *appears behind the two* GIRLS. *He throws a shape and grins*.)

PORTER: Howya girls?

GIRLS: (*Together*) Fuck off.

(*They approach the door again and queue behind* ARTHUR.)

FRONTIER GUARD: (*Points*) And the sweatshirt, not allowed. Strict rule that, you need a shirt to get in here now.

(ARTHUR *looks behind at the* GIRLS *queuing*.)

ARTHUR: So if I had a shirt . . . any shirt?

FRONTIER GUARD: There'd be no problem.

ARTHUR: (*Turning to* FRIEND) Hey, do us a favour. Lend us your blouse for a moment.

FRIEND: Shag off, will you. (*Calls*.) Frank?

ARTHUR: (*To* GIRL) How about you? I'll give it back to you inside.

GIRL: What would I wear?

ARTHUR: Straight swap. (*Grins*.) Come on. Chance it.

(*He peals off his T-shirt and holds it out to her. The* GIRL *looks at her* FRIEND *and then back at him before she unbuttons her blouse and hands it to him*.)

Thanks. (*Puts it on and buttons it up. Turns*.) Bit tight, but it will do. Well . . . any other objections?

FRONTIER GUARD: What the . . .? Don't get fresh with me, right. I work out every day.

ARTHUR: Weights?

FRONTIER GUARD: Weights, press-ups, sprints, you name it. So watch yourself.

ARTHUR: Can you . . . ? Naw, it's a bit hard.

FRONTIER GUARD: Do what? I can do it.

ARTHUR: Naw, it's . . . tough.

FRONTIER GUARD: Don't get fresh. Two hours a day. I can do it.

ARTHUR: Press the back of your left hand flat against your left shoulder. You need to be superfit, mind you.

FRONTIER GUARD: Bullshit, I'll show you.

(*He begins to press his hand backwards.*)

ARTHUR: Right against the shoulder.

(*The* GIRL *looks at him and begins to grin. The* FRIEND *hushes her.* ARTHUR *steps past through the doorway. The* FRONTIER GUARD *is now standing in cartoon camp-gay position. The* PORTER *drunkenly approaches behind his back, looks at him and staggers on through the doorway.*)

FRONTIER GUARD: (*Snapping hand down as he realizes he's been had*) Cheeky bastard. He won't get out so easy. I'll wait till Tommy comes on. We'll sort him. (*Turns to the* GIRLS.) What do you want now?

FRIEND: Frank. She didn't mean it . . . what she said. Can we get in?

FRONTIER GUARD: (*Nods his head towards door*) Go on.

(*The* FRIEND *slips past him and as the* GIRL *is about to follow, the* FRONTIER GUARD *puts his hand out to block her.*)

(*To* FRIEND) Go on. I just want a few words with your friend here in the silly jacket.

GIRL: Sharon, don't. Wait.

FRONTIER GUARD: Go on, she'll be in in a minute. Go on or I'll bar you.

(*The* FRIEND *vanishes. The* FRONTIER GUARD *turns to the* GIRL.)

Think you're smart, do you? Anything else you want to take off? Don't let me stop you.

GIRL: No, I'm . . . (*Almost a whisper*) sorry.

FRONTIER GUARD: What did you say?

GIRL: (*Quietly*) Said, I'm sorry.

FRONTIER GUARD: Can't hear you.

GIRL: I'm sorry for what I said.

FRONTIER GUARD: You be nice to Frank and Frank will be nice to you. (*Puts his arm around her as she tries to wriggle free.*) One kiss for Frank, show that we're pals.

GIRL: Listen, I have to join my friend.

FRONTIER GUARD: She'll wait. Just one. On the cheek, go on.

(*He holds her more firmly.*)

GIRL: Please.

FRONTIER GUARD: One.

(*She reluctantly kisses him slightly on the cheek and shivers. She darts from his arms and tries to avoid his hand on her backside as she gets past.*)

All the same, you girls. See you on the way out, love.

(*She passes through the door as the music soars.* ARTHUR *and the* FRIEND *come forward.* ARTHUR *has the blouse in his hand.*)

FRIEND: Go on, give it back to her.

(ARTHUR *throws her blouse across to her.*)

Give him his thing. God knows what germs . . .

(*The* GIRL *takes off the sweatshirt, waits a minute then throws it across to* ARTHUR. *They look at each other for a moment before the* FRIEND *pulls her away.*)

(*Whispering*) Jesus, you almost blew it again. I'm sick of getting you out of scraps.

GIRL: But he . . .

FRIEND: Leave him for Tommy and Frank.

(*They are caught up in the sweep of music and the* PORTER *and the* FRONTIER GUARD *bounce forward, holding masks and dancing. The* GIRLS *join them, swaying back and forth with masks. The music dips slightly as the* GIRLS *stop and, holding the masks at arms length, confer briefly.*)

GIRL: What's he like?

FRIEND: Big-headed. You know what they say, big head, small . . .

(She gestures with her hands and they laugh, starting to sway again to the louder music. ARTHUR has re-emerged from the back of the stage to stare around him. His eye finally stops on the GIRL and he walks towards her. He taps his mask on her shoulder. The GIRL sees him and flicks the mask away, where it is caught by the PORTER. She stands in an aggressive stance. Her FRIEND is looking over her shoulder at her. The music dips again.)

ARTHUR: Excuse me.

GIRL: What do you want?

ARTHUR: Just to dance.

GIRL: Why?

ARTHUR: I didn't know you needed a reason when I used to dance here.

GIRL: You do now. They're going to get you, you know. Frank's just waiting for his mate to come in.

ARTHUR: I'll be gone before then. Only wanted a look. Used to dance here once. Come on, one dance.

GIRL: *(Doubtful.)* One dance?

(She nods suddenly and they begin to dance. She tries to size him up as they dance.)

You're old for in here . . . are you married?

(He laughs and shakes his head.)

If me mate sees me with you again she'll think I'm after your pension.

ARTHUR: Who gives a toss what people think?

(They continue dancing for a moment.)

GIRL: You dance well for an old fellow.

ARTHUR: The Black-and-Tans taught us the steps when I was young.

(She laughs and they begin to move together. They are drawn closer together but the GIRL pulls back again for a moment before being drawn onwards in the dance.)

GIRL: You were funny . . . with Frank . . . the hand.

ARTHUR: Saw an old Turk do it to a German foreman. Whole

23

factory line stopped work, everybody cracking up. Eventually the foreman joined in as well . . . then they split the old Turk's head open.

(*As the music stops they are left cold, paralysed for a moment in their stances. Her* FRIEND *calls over to her.*)

FRIEND: Kathy!

(*The* GIRL *looks back at her* FRIEND, *suddenly embarrassed.*) Are you coming – (*Points.*) – or what?

(*The* FRIEND *is staring at* ARTHUR. *She looks back at the mask in her hand and flicks it away as her voice grows protective.*)

Come on, will you!

(*The* GIRL *suddenly shrugs* ARTHUR's *hand from her shoulder.*)

GIRL: (*In a low voice to* ARTHUR) No, it's crazy.

ARTHUR: What?

GIRL: Find somebody your own age.

ARTHUR: Age isn't important. Only for horses and greyhounds. Listen . . .

GIRL: (*Confused, crying out*) Please. Can't you see. It *is* for me!

ARTHUR: (*Stepping back*) I'm sorry. I didn't . . . I'm sorry.

(*She turns to walk back towards her* FRIEND *and they exit as the music begins again and* ARTHUR *moves backwards away from her, looking older now, turning and walking tiredly away towards the back of the stage. The music suddenly stops and the four* DANCERS *turn as one and rush towards the front of the stage, shouting together the word* 'Taxi!' ARTHUR *joins end of queue as the voices jumble together.*)

PORTER: No, he's not getting sick, he always walks like that.

FRONTIER GUARD: I was here first, mate. Shove over there.

FRIEND: Please, Clondalkin, there's two of us.

GIRL: (*Back at the* FRONTIER GUARD) Quit pushing, will you.

PORTER: Just up to . . . shag it.

(*They watch the taxi move off into the distance.* GIRL *sees* ARTHUR *and edges back towards the* FRIEND. ARTHUR *glances at her as he walks away.*)

FRIEND: (*Joking*) You need a minder. Bleeding geriatric he
    was. Are you trying to get us a bad name? I mean he has
    the free travel and all, but . . .

GIRL: Ah just leave him alone, will you.

FRIEND: Ah well, at least you could have brought him home
    to meet your Da unlike those two punks we met last week.
    Himself and your Da could have had a great time reminis-
    cing about the Emergency and rationing . . .

GIRL: Give over, Sharon, he beat the creep you were dancing
    with.

FRIEND: At least my fellow had his own teeth.

GIRL: Sharon, you make everything so . . .
    (*She stops moving and speaking when she suddenly glimpses*
    ARTHUR *in the distance.*)

FRIEND: I'd love a burger.
    (*Stage dissolves into burger hut scene with voices together.*)

PORTER: Double Kuntucky vomit burger with stale fries. I'm
    only messing, honest.

FRONTIER GUARD: I'm waiting here half the night.

FRIEND: Shift your hand or I'll burst you.

GIRL: I don't want a burger, Sharon.
    (ARTHUR *passes to the far side of the stage. The* GIRL *turns*
    and glimpses him. He mimes pulling a jacket tighter around
    himself, leans on the wall of the imaginary quay, facing the
    audience and sighs as he stares down. Once or twice, he
    shakes his head.)

GIRL: Sharon, there he is by the river. Just wait for me . . . a
    minute.

FRIEND: Don't be thick, Kathy, come on will you.

GIRL: I just want to say goodbye to him.

FRIEND: There's Jimmy's parked outside the Savoy, he'll give
    us a lift. I'm going now.

GIRL: (*As the* FRIEND *moves*) Sharon . . .
    (*She hesitantly begins to approach* ARTHUR. *She pauses at*
    his back as he tries to clear his ears and then taps him on the
    shoulder. She jumps back as he turns. He raises his hand to
    his head and shakes it again.)

You got out OK, I was worried . . .

ARTHUR: What, the bouncer? I'd called his bluff first time.

GIRL: (*Looking at him*) Are you . . . ?

ARTHUR: (*After a moment*) The disco. It's the hissing . . . like being underwater for a while when you come out.

GIRL: You mustn't be used to it.

ARTHUR: I'm not. It's been a long time since I was in there. And it was all live music then. I was there the night the police raided it when the Chosen Few were playing. I was only fourteen, but I was there. I saw Gallagher with the Impact and Skid Row . . .

GIRL: (*With increasing incomprehension*) Who?

ARTHUR: (*Looks at her*) Skid . . . (*Stops.*) Just bands.

GIRL: Oh.

(*He looks out towards the audience. She follows his eyes.*)

The river, it's nice at night, disguised like.

ARTHUR: Do they still tell you at school, about O'Connell Street? The widest street in Europe, they used to say.

GIRL: (*Surprised at the question*) Don't know. (*Shrugs her shoulders.*) I never listened to them.

ARTHUR: 'The widest street.' I used to believe them. That same old Turk said it to me once, about his village. But it's true of here too.

GIRL: (*Puzzled*) What is?

ARTHUR: It's all smaller, different when you return. Look at it . . . O'Connell Street. Just like some honky-tonk provincial plaza. Everywhere closed except the burger huts, all the buses gone, everyone milling around drunk, taking to the glittering lights like aborigines to whiskey. Just like some provincial kip I've seen dozens of. (*Pauses.*) But it all seemed so grand once. As a kid I remember . . . being choked up, staring down at it, as far as the eye could see . . . as a treat from the Pillar.

GIRL: The what?

ARTHUR: Nelson's.

GIRL: Jesus, I wasn't born when that was blown up . . . (*Suddenly embarrassed*) Sorry, it must make you feel . . .

26

ARTHUR: (*Quietly*) No, I deserve it. I'm talking too much.

GIRL: I keep doing that, don't I?

ARTHUR: No, you're right.

GIRL: (*Hesitantly*) I didn't mean to hurt you.

(*The* PORTER *enters, singing in drunken fashion.* ARTHUR *and the* GIRL *turn to look at him.*)

PORTER: Giz a cigarette.

ARTHUR: Sorry, mate, I haven't any.

(*The* PORTER *leans on the barrel and lowers his head.*)

PORTER: Giz a cigarette, go on, will you.

ARTHUR: Sorry, mate, I told you, I haven't any.

PORTER: Go on, giz . . .

ARTHUR: Go on back. You'll meet somebody.

GIRL: No. I've had enough. I hate it. My friend's annoyed with me anyway, she's gone on.

ARTHUR: How will you get home?

GIRL: I'll get a taxi. I have the money.

ARTHUR: I'll take you home if you let me.

(*The* GIRL *looks at him uncertainly.*)

GIRL: Have you a car?

(*He grins and shakes his head as they begin to walk towards the right.*)

ARTHUR: No, we're out of miracles – there was a run of them earlier. I've a motorbike, bought it when I came home. Broke me, but shag it. Couldn't afford one when I was growing up. Always swore I'd get one, roar down all the lanes I knew as a kid. It's stupid, I suppose. Bread and margarine till I get work, but you'd get a pain in your hole being sensible. Do you want to risk it?

GIRL: I survived the dancing clones. I'd say I'll survive it. It has an engine at least?

ARTHUR: This thing would take you across the Sahara Desert.

GIRL: Will it get us to Clondalkin?

ARTHUR: Jaysus, I'd sooner chance the Sahara Desert, but we'll give it a lash. Here, mind your man.

(*The* PORTER *raises his head from the barrel at the right of*

27

stage. He sways forward, wheeling it, singing, then plonks it down, leans on it and looks at them.) ARTHUR *leads the* GIRL *over towards where the imaginary bike is parked and the* FRONTIER GUARD *and the* FRIEND *emerge from the left.*)

FRONTIER GUARD: Ruined the play, darling. There was no need to say that at the interval, just because he was wearing jeans at the theatre.

FRIEND: All I asked him was why wasn't he out minding the cars.

FRONTIER GUARD: (*Producing car keys*) He was a member of the audience, love. He was just wearing jeans.

FRIEND: Well he looked like the lad in the cap you gave the 50p to.

FRONTIER GUARD: Oh, my God!

(*He walks the length of the stage, searching, then turns and darts back the way he has come. The* FRIEND *follows him.*)

ARTHUR: The bike is here by the monument.

(*There is a motorcycle helmet at the back of the stage, which* ARTHUR *and the* GIRL *stop at. The drunk* PORTER *wanders back to them.*)

PORTER: Is the last 19 gone?

ARTHUR: (*Bending down for the helmet*) Gone. Gone, mate. It's after twelve.

PORTER: The last 22?

ARTHUR: They're all gone.

PORTER: The 16s or the 3s?

ARTHUR: (*Straightening with helmet*) All the buses are in bed. It's safe to cross the road.

(*The drunk* PORTER *has swayed across the stage, catching hold of the raised platform which almost falls on his head.* ARTHUR *takes it from him so that it lies on its side.*)

FRONTIER GUARD: Oh, my God. Darling!

FRIEND: What?

FRONTIER GUARD: The Volvo. The new Volvo is gone. (*To* ARTHUR) You there, excuse me. My new Volvo is gone. It was there. Did you see . . . ?

ARTHUR: No, I'm sorry, mate. Just after coming along.

PORTER: (*To* ARTHUR) What's wrong with him? What's up?

ARTHUR: His flash Volvo. It's gone.

PORTER: (*Moving over to* FRONTIER GUARD) Your last Rolo? It's gone. Here, I'll give you a hand looking. You look there . . .

(*He begins to search while the* FRONTIER GUARD *and the* FRIEND *stand back in horror from him. They quickly walk off and the* PORTER *follows them.*)

Here, I'll take a lift off you.

(ARTHUR *hands the helmet to the* GIRL.)

GIRL: Have you only one helmet? What about you?

ARTHUR: Take it.

(*The* GIRL *looks at it in his hands and then takes it and raises it over her head as her recorded voice begins to speak. They stand for a moment as if astride the bike and the lights move to suggest speed with slots of white as they pass beneath lamp-posts.*)

GIRL'S VOICE:

> I accepted it like a pledge
> And my arms circled your leather jacket
> > Your hair blown into my face
> We raced up the quays towards my estate.

> Down a lane choked with scrap
> Among the rust-eaten ghosts of lorries
> > Within sight of my father's house
> Is where I first loved Arthur Cleary.

(*The engine dies with the last line of the poem. The* GIRL *gets off the bike and turns to face* ARTHUR. *He goes to help her remove the helmet but then she steps back, defining her territory. She takes the helmet off, waits a moment, then throws it over to him. She fixes her hair and looks at him. They are both silent as if in their private thoughts.* ARTHUR *leans on the edge of the platform.*)

ARTHUR: That disco. I was stupid to go back. It used to be

my regular. It was crazy to think the same people might be there, but they all seem to have vanished. It was one of the few places I knew that was still standing. I suppose they're all married by now. Mortgages, ulcers, overdrafts. Far from dancing on their minds.

GIRL: Where were you?

ARTHUR: Places . . . all much the same, you forget the names.

GIRL: Glad to be back?

ARTHUR: Just got to get my bearings. You know, feels like only months I was away and yet you keep turning corners and what should be there isn't there. Sorry, I really am talking too much.

GIRL: No.

ARTHUR: Great place to talk, that's how I remember it. Meeting people, hours passing, evenings, winding up in rooms still talking. Funny – say hello to people now they look at you. Think it's all I've said in the last week – ten fags, milk, the paper, *zwei Brötchen und einige Käse* – they look at you like you've ten heads – oh Jaysus, sorry, a scabby sliced pan, please.

GIRL: You're funny.

ARTHUR: How do you mean?

GIRL: Don't know . . . different. (*Pause.*) Why'd you come back to this kip?

ARTHUR: I belong in this kip. It's like at the end of a night, you know, you have to go home.

GIRL: You're welcome to it. If I had a chance I would be gone tomorrow. Anywhere – just out of here. Somewhere anonymous, the freedom of some city where if you walked down the longest street not one person would care who you are or where you're from.

ARTHUR: That can be lonely too.

GIRL: You can live with loneliness. You can't live here. (*Climbs awkwardly on to the top of the barrel and looks at him.*) You're different somehow, you're still breathing. Maybe because you got out. Sometimes . . . don't laugh . . . sometimes I think they've sucked all the air out of this city and people are walking around opening and closing their mouths with nothing coming in and nothing going out. (*Blushes and laughs, jumping down in embarrassment.*) And that sounds crazy, I know.

ARTHUR: No. Some nights working in a canning factory in Denmark I'd stand up on the loading bay beside the hoist and I'd look down at three in the morning on the workers below, nobody speaking, the limbs moving automatically, the curious stillness behind all the bustle. And I'd start thinking it was the conveyor belt and the loading machine that were alive, that they were thinking more cans for the arms, and at seven in the morning the machines would stop and the arms of the men would move back and forth till somebody remembered to press a switch. So maybe I'm crazy too, but that's why I came home.

(*The* GIRL *approaches him. She lifts her arms, then folds them behind her back. He does the same. They repeat the action again.*)

ARTHUR: (*Hesitantly*) How . . . old . . . ?

GIRL: Eighteen. (*Pause.*) And you?

ARTHUR: (*After a moment*) Thirty-five.

(*She walks behind the platform in embarrassment and leans on it.*)

GIRL: (*Softly*) You don't think I'm a slut?

(*He smiles and shakes his head.*)

You're not a queer, are you?

(*He laughs.*)

ARTHUR: No. (*Laughs again.*) Why do you ask?

GIRL: Don't know. I suppose . . . well, you haven't tried anything. (*Quickly*) Not that I want you to, like . . . but often lads can be pushy, like, just want to get you out by yourself and then get away.

ARTHUR: So did I once. So did every man.

(*The* GIRL *comes back around to face him.*)

GIRL: You won't take the wrong idea about me?

ARTHUR: I'll only take whatever idea you want.

GIRL: (*Leaning her face towards him*) Will you . . . ?

(*They embrace and kiss. There is a subtle interplay of lights to suggest time passing. Lights return to normal as the* GIRL *turns around so that she is still in* ARTHUR'*s arms but facing away from him. They are both silent as if in their private thoughts.*)

ARTHUR: It was the strangest thing.

GIRL: (*Looks up.*) What?

ARTHUR: The church. Near the flats. There was such an overspill of people living there that they put up a temporary one. The tin one they called it – a sort of huge prefab. Inside as a child you'd hear the rain splattering against the corrugated-tin roof. I'd forgotten that sound till one winter in a Dutch factory . . . sleeping in those long iron dormitories, the Turks, the Moluccans, the first few of the Irish. I'd wake at night and remember . . . like it would always be there, part of me . . . to return to. (*Stops.*) First night I got home I went walking, buildings boarded up, new names over shops. I came to the lane where the church had been. There was a crackling sound, then I smelt the smoke. They were clearing the site. There were just the girders of the church left and everything else still smouldering, waiting to be shifted. Hadn't been there or any other church since I was fifteen. But it was in my mind as something that would never change.

(*Listening to him, the* GIRL *suddenly shivers and steps away.*)

ARTHUR: (*Concerned*) What's wrong?

GIRL: (*Retreating towards the barrel*) I don't know. You know that feeling like this has happened before. Suddenly . . . it scared me.

ARTHUR: Shush . . . it will be dawn soon. Did you ever wait up for the dawn?

(*The* GIRL *shakes her head.*)

(*Approaching her*) So strange, you're exhausted, you can't go on, and then . . . felt it on so many nights working in factories . . . the first hint of light and you can feel it through your body, energy, from nowhere, strength you

didn't know you had from deep within you . . . Then the
light comes and it floods you. Hey . . .

GIRL: What?

ARTHUR: Never thought I'd . . . feel new again, like now . . .

GIRL: (*Moving away, this time behind the platform which she
leans on*) Arthur, I don't want to hear . . . you scare me, I
don't always understand you . . . you don't talk like real
people.

ARTHUR: Real people?

(*Silently the* PORTER *and the* FRIEND *emerge on stage.
The* PORTER *stands at the front left while the* FRIEND,
*who has donned a mask, stands with her back to the audi-
ence.*)

GIRL: You know what I mean . . . safe. (*Points.*) See that
house, with the light still on?

ARTHUR: (*Looking*) Yeah.

GIRL: That's his light, will burn till I go in. Never been this
late before. He'll be worried . . . listening for me. It's
funny . . . when I was young and he was working. (*A
pause as she looks down at her hands.*) He talked like you
. . . like he wasn't scared of looking over his shoulder . . .
like . . .

(*The* PORTER *suddenly turns, his face white with anger, his
hands clenched.* ARTHUR *retreats to edge of stage.*)

PORTER: And now you're taking up with this fellow, this
knacker.

GIRL: He's not, Dad.

PORTER: Well, whatever he is, he's too old for you. Can't you
see child, he's no job, he's got nothing. Good Christ, I
worked hard enough all these years to try and get you
something, to try and lift you up. Where's he going,
where can he bring you? Some corporation flat. You're
only a child yet. You're throwing your life away for him.

GIRL: It's not serious, Dad. I'm not even sure about him. It's
just that he's . . . different. There's something . . .

PORTER: Different! May be different to you but I've seen his
like all my life. Every week there'd be another one of them

in the factory and within the month they'd be gone. Fly-boys. Drifters. Only certainty was that they'd be gone. How could he build a life for you like I've tried to build for your mother? Tell me that, how? A knacker in a leather jacket, with one hand longer than the other and the rattle of his bike waking the street at every hour of the night. What's so special about him then?

GIRL: (*Crying out suddenly*) He's not dead! He's not beaten! He's . . .

PORTER: (*Quietly*) Like I am, is it? Beaten?

(*There is a pause while the mood changes. Then the* GIRL *speaks quietly.*)

GIRL: Do you remember, Dad? Bull Island?

(*The* PORTER *smiles ruefully.*)

The thrill of hiding up there in the sand dunes waiting for you to find me, peering out at you climbing up. Remember?

PORTER: I'd park the car on the strand and you'd be gone before my back was turned. Always running. A proper little rascal.

(*The* GIRL *suddenly runs over to the far side of the stage with childish strides. She hides behind the barrel as he comes looking for her. She runs out, avoiding him and then, looking over her shoulder, stands for a moment with hands clenched, giggling. He circles her and when she tries to run he catches her and throws her up in his arms. She shouts for him to let her go and he lowers her on to the floor where she puts her feet on his shoes so that when he pulls her up again she is dancing with him like a child with her father. A note of sadness enters his voice.*)

That was a good car that. I kept it well.

GIRL: You'll have a car again, Dad. Only a matter of time.

(*The* PORTER *lets her go, looking down at his hands in a gesture of futility.*)

You looked after us well, Dad. You still do.

PORTER: Feel so useless, love. Wish I was dead sometimes. You'd have the insurance then at least.

GIRL: (*Crying out as she runs to him*) Daddy, don't say that. Don't wish it. You're the best.

PORTER: (*Lifting his hands to examine them, then pulls the platform back up and pushes it into place fiercely as he speaks.*) I've good hands. Can make things with these. Give me wood and I'll make it. Tables, chairs, shelves. I never thought I'd be idle with these. A skill for life they said. Always find something.

GIRL: It doesn't matter, Daddy. You've done so much, all your life. It's time to rest now.

PORTER: The women cried the day we left. Out in the open at the gates of the factory. The television were there. All the fuss, the papers. Then they left us alone. With just our thoughts. (*Lights fade on him and the GIRL and rise on ARTHUR who is now standing beside the barrel and on the FRIEND who has turned with the mask still over her face. ARTHUR turns slowly till he is facing her in silhouette.*)

ARTHUR: Ma. I know you can't hear, but I'll talk to you still. You have to talk to someone.

FRIEND: I know, son. I talked to you often enough those years you were abroad.

ARTHUR: I was never one for writing, Ma.

FRIEND: Never expected you to, son. You had your own life.

ARTHUR: She's so much younger than me, Ma. All the lads I knew, they're all gone. The girls with prams, so suddenly old.

FRIEND: (*Softly*) Fifteen years, son. A sorrowful decade and a half.

ARTHUR: We had our joyful one.

FRIEND: (*Ironic as she slowly lowers the mask*) How often did I see you on your knees telling your beads?

ARTHUR: (*Laughs*) As often as I saw you.

FRIEND: Still, we had our good times.

ARTHUR: Mornings I'd climb down the steps from these flats and people would shout, 'Arthur Cleary! Arthur Cleary! Come in! Come in!'

FRIEND: Me laughing from the balcony at your mates trying to dance like Zorba the Greek.

(ARTHUR *puts his hands out on to two imaginary shoulders and moves his body in the motions of a Greek dance.*)

ARTHUR: Closing time Fridays walking up from town, playing football in the traffic. Remember I'd bring you a baby Power and we'd sit round drinking bottles of Guinness from brown-paper bags.

FRIEND: At three in the morning, they'd still be arriving. Is that Arthur Cleary's? Have we found the place?

ARTHUR: This is the place, but now I can't find them. Ma, I can't find you. I can't find my old self. Feel so old ... except when she's beside me.

(*There is a pause to suggest time passing.*)

Mrs Burke told me, Ma, how you lived out those last years on white bread and tea.

FRIEND: They barred me from the pub son, when the new owners did it up. Barred when I was the first woman who refused to be corralled inside the snug years before. Singing, they said I was. What's a pub for, only singing?

ARTHUR: You broke your hip trying to cross the road when that security van ran the lights.

FRIEND: Shagging Culchie drivers.

ARTHUR: I wasn't running from you, Ma. You know that, don't you?

(*She doesn't answer.*)

It was just ... the time. So easy to drift between jobs and places, it just seemed right to wander off for a while and then wander back. Only I never did. Oh, I often imagined it, arriving back, no warning, nothing, just being there at dawn with a bottle of brandy and the stubble of three days' travel. (*Quietly*) Only it wasn't like that, was it?

FRIEND: You've never been to the grave, son. Though I was never there myself before I went to keep him company in it.

ARTHUR: Had a drink for you, Ma, instead. Knew you'd prefer that. Among the disco lights and the canned music. And sang 'Who Fears to Speak of Easter Week?' for you. The owner almost shat himself. I think he thought I was cracked.

FRIEND: When did we ever give a shite what any of them thought of us, son?

ARTHUR: When did we ever, Ma? (*Pause.*) Why am I talking to you, Ma? The dead cannot talk.

FRIEND: They can, son. But only among themselves.

(*The* FRIEND *raises the mask to her face and turns away as* ARTHUR *looks back, suddenly frightened. The* GIRL *moves over to the* PORTER *and embraces his back, her hand resting momentarily on his shoulder, her lips lightly touching the back of his neck. He acknowledges the embrace by resting his head back for a moment against hers. She then goes to the side of the stage and picks up the helmet. The* GIRL *and* ARTHUR *meet in the centre of the stage.* ARTHUR *approaches her cautiously and she hands him back the helmet. He stares at it for a moment, then turns and walks off, leaving it down on the side of the stage. The* FRIEND *runs on to the front of the stage and sits on the box. The* GIRL *approaches her.*)

Did you say goodbye to him, like we agreed?

GIRL: I did. (*Sits on the box as well.*) He was waiting for me along the quays, staring at the water like he always did. Didn't think I'd have the courage. 'Arthur, I'm sorry,' I said. 'It's just too big a gap, it's not right.' He never spoke, Sharon, his face looked old, suddenly, like all the air had drained from it.

FRIEND: I know it's hard. You were fairly gone on him but it's for the best. You'll see. It'll be like old times again.

(*The* FRIEND *rises and the* GIRL *follows her.*)

GIRL: All the way home, felt like throwing myself from the bus. I came in, Sharon, saw my father, just sitting staring at the box. And I remembered a man who feared no other, a brown wage packet left on an oilskinned table. If he could only cry, I could stay with him, but his kind were never taught how to show grief. I need to learn to breathe. Sharon, I need Arthur and I don't know how to ask, to teach me . . . to wake up and not be afraid of what the day will bring. (*Pause.*) I've packed a bag, Sharon. If he'll take

37

me in I'll go to him, or I'll go somewhere else, anywhere, but I don't fit here any more. (*Pause.*) Will you be glad for me?

FRIEND: What's wrong with here?

GIRL: You hate it, you always say you do.

FRIEND: But I'll settle for it. I'm not running half-cocked after anybody. Real life isn't like that. This isn't a bleeding movie, Kathy, real people don't do this. You're even starting to talk like that header.

GIRL: I can't breathe here, Sharon.

FRIEND: Have you ever tried opening and closing your mouth? For God's sake, Kathy, your man's a fossil and he doesn't need to breathe. You're just walking out, leaving me.

GIRL: Not you, I'll see you the same, just . . .

FRIEND: How could it be the same . . . you, me and him? Been calling for you since I was five . . . for school, dances, mitching out, covering up for you. And you say it will be the same. We were never good enough for you, isn't that right?

GIRL: Sharon, please.

FRIEND: You'll beg for one of these houses one day. You'll settle for a squawling brat and yellow pack bread and a thrill off the fridge, if you're lucky. Just like the rest of us.

GIRL: I'm going, Sharon.

FRIEND: Go on then and good luck, kid. 'Cause I won't know you when you come running back in a week's time with your tail between your legs. Do you hear?

(*The* FRIEND *storms off-stage and the* GIRL *is left alone as the* PORTER *walks silently past. The recorded voice is heard.*)

GIRL'S VOICE: I had a room with fresh linen
                 And parents to watch over me
                 A brown dog slept at my feet
                 I left them for Arthur Cleary.

(*When the lights rise they suggest dawn.* ARTHUR *is still*

38

standing at the edge of the stage. He has a bunch of keys in his hand. The GIRL *approaches and stands a few feet away from him, speaking to his back.*)

GIRL: Been walking all night, round and round these flats. (*Pause.*) I left, Arthur. Am I crazy or what?

(*Neither speaks for a moment.*)

ARTHUR: I don't know. And I don't care, except you're here.

(*He throws her the keys and, as she comes forward, they embrace. The lights go down and the sinister music from the first* FRONTIER GUARD *border scene returns. When a weak light returns it is shining above* ARTHUR's *head as he stands against the wooden platform with the* PORTER *shining his torch up and down the bars from behind. The* FRONTIER GUARD *approaches and shines his torch at* ARTHUR's *face.*)

FRONTIER GUARD: Passport please.

(ARTHUR *recovers.*)

ARTHUR: Oh, sorry.

(*He hands him a passport which the* FRONTIER GUARD *opens and examines.*)

FRONTIER GUARD: Ah Irish. Boom-boom! Eh!

(*He laughs.*)

ARTHUR: Yeah. Boom-bleeding-boom.

(*The* FRONTIER GUARD *hands him back the passport.*)

Eh? Where am I now? Which side of the border am I on?

FRONTIER GUARD: What does it matter to you, Irish? Either side you are a long way from home.

ARTHUR: (*Shrugs his head towards the light behind him*) What's he looking at the wheels for?

FRONTIER GUARD: Looking for? (*Laughs.*) It is the rules, Irish. We will go on soon.

(*He turns to leave him.*)

ARTHUR: (*Suddenly puzzled*) Wait, have you . . . eh, have you checked my passport before?

(*The* FRONTIER GUARD *returns, shining torch at* ARTHUR.)

FRONTIER GUARD: Before? We only check once.

ARTHUR: Well then, do I know you from somewhere?

FRONTIER GUARD: Maybe you take this train before, Irish?

ARTHUR: No, somewhere else. Somewhere different.

FRONTIER GUARD: You know a brothel called BB's in Stuttgart?

ARTHUR: No.

FRONTIER GUARD: Neither do I! (*Laughs heartily.*) Funny, eh?

ARTHUR: I do know you. Wait.

(*He looks closely at the man who shrugs his shoulders and walks behind the platform. Suddenly the* PORTER *and himself begin to sing in a Dublin accent.*)

FRONTIER GUARD *and* PORTER: Ah poor old Dicey Riley, she has taken to the sup, sup, sup!

(*The* FRONTIER GUARD *comes back around and stares at* ARTHUR. *He holds his hand out and speaks in his Deignan voice.*)

FRONTIER GUARD: Hey, wait a minute. (*Shakes his hand.*) I know you.

(*Reverting back to the* FRONTIER GUARD *he walks back behind platform, leaving* ARTHUR *confused and frightened.*)

FRONTIER GUARD *and* PORTER: (*Out of sight*) Poor oul Dicey Riley, she will never give it up!

(*The lights go back, there is a banging and as they rise the* PORTER *scarpers, with child-like steps across the stage to exit at far side. The* FRONTIER GUARD *emerges with a leather book in his hand – which he has been banging on the wooden supports of the stage – and shouts.*)

FRONTIER GUARD: Frankie! Young Frankie Doyle! I see you there, I'm no fool, you know. Come back here, tell your mother I want to see her.

(ARTHUR *has turned to stand on the left side of platform with his hands around the* GIRL. *The* FRONTIER GUARD *turns from looking after the* PORTER *to face an imaginary door and shouts.*)

I know you're in there, Mrs Doyle! I'm not a fool you know. If you can't pay them, you shouldn't take out loans. (*He consults his ledger.*) Didn't I see young Frankie from the car driving up to the flats? Three weeks, Mrs Doyle, three weeks. God would have made the world three times. You think that husband of yours could have made three pounds even. Easy knowing the creator of heaven and earth didn't come from this block of flats.

(*The* FRIEND *emerges on right side of stage.*)

(*Politely to the* FRIEND *as he turns*) Ah, Mrs Burke. Fine weather.

FRIEND: The better for not being in your clutches, Mr Deignan.

FRONTIER GUARD: Always here to help, Mrs Burke.

FRIEND: Go and shite.

(*She exits.*)

FRONTIER GUARD: (*Smiles after her*) Charming.

(*The* FRONTIER GUARD *sees* ARTHUR *and the* GIRL, *and looks down his ledger dismissively as he speaks.*)

Eh, what are you at then?

(ARTHUR *and the* GIRL *ignore him.*)

Headtheball, I'm talking to you!

ARTHUR: (*Quietly, still looking at the door*) I live here.

FRONTIER GUARD: Since when? Old Mrs Cleary used to live there.

ARTHUR: (*Turning*) I was born here.

FRONTIER GUARD: Tell me another. I've had me eye on that place since the oul bat died. A troublesome oul biddy she was too. This law and that law.

(*He snorts.*)

ARTHUR: (*Quietly, still not looking at him*) Nice to know my mother had such a concerned friend.

FRONTIER GUARD: (*Snaps fingers*) Wait a minute. I have you. Arthur! Arthur Cleary! Sure, wasn't I a year behind you in school? Deignan, Larry Deignan. My mother had the shop on the corner. Sure, I used to look up to you. Only the mother, you know, wasn't too keen. (*Pause.*) So, the famous son, eh, the wanderer.

ARTHUR: Will you stop.

(*The* FRONTIER GUARD *approaches.*)

FRONTIER GUARD: No offence meant, Arthur. I thought you were just squatters. You get some dodgy types around here. (*Puts out his hand.*)

ARTHUR: (*Ignoring his hand*) So I see.

FRONTIER GUARD: Don't know what brought you back. Great to see you all the same. Do you remember . . . the day you had to be dug out of old McCarthy the teacher, the day you were expelled from school? God, you were a legend then. You remember me, Arthur? Don't you? And the mother? The little shop on the corner. Here, I'll give you my card. I could be of use to you settling in.

ARTHUR: (*Ignoring his hand, he finds the keys.*) I remember the firelighter.

FRONTIER GUARD: (*Bewildered*) The what?

ARTHUR: The young tinker lad my mother gave a threepenny bit to once. He went looking for sweets in your mother's shop. She gave him a firelighter and a penny change. He thought it was coconut and stuffed it in his mouth. You must remember him now, you were laughing about it long enough. Never able to speak again. I used to see him begging near the Four Courts. It will teach his sort a lesson, your mother always said. (*He gives a slight laugh.*) Yeah, I remember her well.

(FRONTIER GUARD *moves in close as if about to strike* ARTHUR, *then gives a little laugh.*)

FRONTIER GUARD: Always the jokes Arthur, eh? I'll leave you my card. It will be a pleasure hearing from you.

(*He presses it into* ARTHUR's *hand and exits.* ARTHUR *looks at it, then tears it up and exits into where the flat would be. The* GIRL, *who has been leaning on the platform during this, now comes forward and, carefully picking up the pieces of the card, stares at them before exiting with them held in her hand.*)

ACT TWO

A motorbike engine is heard for a moment in the darkness before the engine is switched off, and the soundtrack takes on a rural nature as the lights come up. There is a shout before ARTHUR *enters first from the back of the stage at a trot as though coming down a slope and turns to catch the* GIRL *who rushes on after him.*

ARTHUR: No problem to you. I told you so.

GIRL: No problem for you in those boots. The feet are stung off me. There's nettles up there like bamboos.

ARTHUR: We'll soon be rid of those.

(He kneels and, plucking imaginary leaves from ground, begins to rub her lower legs.)

ARTHUR: Dock leaves. Your only men. (*The* GIRL *is looking around her.*) Well, was I right? Knocksedan. Isn't it great?

GIRL: Tell me about it again.

(He stops rubbing and looks up at her.)

ARTHUR: Sure can't you see it with your own eyes?

GIRL: It's not the same. It's only weeds and bushes and rocks, but when you describe it it's special, it's your world.

ARTHUR: (*Looking around him*) It's as much yours as mine. That's what's special about it ... it's just here, it's any-body's.

GIRL: It's not here Arthur. Not the way you knew it. With other people ... well, places seem to pass before them like scenes in a film, but with you it's all kept inside – every-where's special.

43

ARTHUR: It's just a place.

GIRL: All you have are places . . . and the dole.

ARTHUR: We manage.

GIRL: (*Going to sit on barrel*) You're a sap, Arthur Cleary, and I'm worse for going along with you. Tell me about this one. Come on. Who did you come here with?

(ARTHUR *comes over for her to climb on his back. They stand staring out at the audience.*)

ARTHUR: Anyone who would come. Or just alone.

GIRL: Girls?

ARTHUR: Girls who'd go sick from the factories to swim here in the river with me. Two hours getting them to take their dresses off for five minutes in the water. (*Grins.*) But it was worth it. That mound there. (*Points.*) Man-made. Older than Christ. Some evenings I'd climb up there in the dusk and it was as though you could almost hear it saying to you, 'I know you. I know everything you will ever feel. I have felt it all before.'

GIRL: More likely it was saying, 'Stop standing on my skull, you're giving me a headache.' Hills don't talk, Arthur. (*Looks around her again.*) Was this always here?

ARTHUR: Of course.

GIRL: Never saw it or knew it. All these hidden bits of the city . . . (*Her voice changes.*) Six weeks today, Arthur.

ARTHUR: You should go back to see him.

GIRL: Tell him what . . . now I know Knocksedan and the Pigeon House and Howth Head at night and the lanes off Thomas Street. Jesus, Arthur, you couldn't explain that to real people . . . it's not real life, that's what Sharon said.

ARTHUR: What's real life; a clean job, pretending you own some mortgaged house on an estate, death from cancer at forty?

GIRL: That's what Sharon said I'd settle for. This is so good it frightens me . . . (*Taps him on the head as though it was wooden.*) Arthur, are you listening to me?

ARTHUR: I am in my granny. I'm wondering are the logs still down there that you could cross the river by. We'll climb down and have a gander.

GIRL: Jesus, more nettles, more briars.

(ARTHUR *lowers her down his back.*)

ARTHUR: Sure a little prick will do you no harm.

GIRL: Oh, are you coming as well?

(*She runs as he grabs at her in mock anger and chases her towards the edge of the platform which she mounts and, picking up his helmet, she places it back to front on his head. She turns him round and, with a little kick, sends him out into the middle of the stage. Sinister music begins as she retreats and both the* FRONTIER GUARD *and the* PORTER *emerge on to the stage.* ARTHUR *gropes his way forward until his foot hits against the box. He stops and takes the helmet off as the* FRONTIER GUARD *and the* PORTER *form themselves into a queue behind him, slouching down with the look of broken men with long patience.* ARTHUR *is standing facing the barrel, staring around him as if confused at how he got there. The queue moves in a sequence of short mimed jerks, during which* ARTHUR *glances behind him to see the* PORTER. *There is silence for a moment as* ARTHUR *glares around at the* PORTER. *Then he turns again to stare at him. During the ensuing conversation the* FRONTIER GUARD *keeps staring between them.*)

ARTHUR: Johnny, isn't it . . . Johnny Carroll?

(*The* PORTER *looks suspicious and then recognizes him.*)

PORTER: Arthur Cleary? I thought you were off in Germany?

ARTHUR: I was, but I'm back. (*Looks up.*) You'd have thought they would have painted the dole office in my absence. But, come here, I thought you were well in for life up there in McGuirks.

PORTER: I was. Till I was laid off. But that's four years ago. Sure that place is just a crater now. All that row of factories is the same. You can see them from the train with the roofs caved in. There's nothing here now, Arthur. Not like long ago.

ARTHUR: Do you remember, where was it . . . that timber yard off Francis Street? We both started together at nine o'clock. A right hole. We left it at eleven. Told your man to fuck himself.

PORTER: And we were fixed up over in that carton factory in the Combe by lunchtime. Those were the days. There was always a start somewhere. Seems like another world now, walking from one job to the next. If people get in anywhere these days they stick like plasticine.

ARTHUR: (*Thinks.*) Mind you, the carton factory was a hole too. (*Snaps fingers.*) What a weird bunch worked there. Remember – Dockets?

PORTER: (*Mock voice*) Have you a docket for that, son? Have you a docket? (*Normal voice*) And the little guy in the white coat. You could barely see his head over the machines.

ARTHUR: (*Hand over his mouth*) 'Stop walking in that hole.' (*Looks around as if staring over the top of a loin machine.*) Who said that? If I catch the lad who said that he's fired.

PORTER: Remember Boots?

ARTHUR: Boots! For God's sake. I'd forgotten him. Refused to wear anything else, just the one pair day or night. We used to claim he slept in them.

PORTER: You had a song about him, remember? The Elvis voice, up on the pallet of cartons, doing all the movements with the brush. Remember Boots even caught you?

ARTHUR: How did it go?

PORTER: Jaysus, it's a long time.

ARTHUR: Wait. (*Sings in mock Elvis accent*) 'My granny would like to rock and roll.'
(*He points at the PORTER, waiting for response.*)

PORTER: 'But I'm too tired to dig her up.'

ARTHUR *and* PORTER:
    My goldfish woud love a bowl
  'Cause he hates crapping in a cup,
    My wife's abandoned me,
  But I don't care two hoots
    'Cause all I really want to do
  Is stomp around in black rubber wellington boots.

(*The two of them have mimed a dance during the verse to the*

46

increasing bemusement of the FRONTIER GUARD. *Now with their hands impersonating guitars they move in for the kill, moving closer and closer together with each word until the* FRONTIER GUARD *is squashed between them, almost bent double with his hands still in his pockets.*)

'Boots! Boots! Boots! Boots!'

FRONTIER GUARD: (*Ironically, looking at* ARTHUR) The King, eh?

PORTER: The real McCoy. Arthur Cleary.

ARTHUR: That's where we first met Eamon, 'member –

PORTER: The original rocker.

(*He throws shapes.*)

ARTHUR: Suede shoes, the lapels on the jacket, the whole works. Where's he now?

PORTER: (*Quietly*) He's fucking dead, Arthur. He blew his own brains out last year. We're all fucking dead, Arthur, or as good as, in this kip.

ARTHUR: We've a few pints to sink before they lower us down yet. Do you remember the time . . .

PORTER: (*Surly*) No. It's gone.

(*The* FRONTIER GUARD *nudges* ARTHUR *with his shoulder and shouts as if to the rest of the queue.*)

FRONTIER GUARD: Will you hurry fucking up? Some of us have jobs to go to.

ARTHUR: (*Noticing the* FRONTIER GUARD *and speaking to him*) Do I know you, mate?

FRONTIER GUARD: You don't know nothing.

ARTHUR: (*Puzzled*) From somewhere . . . that face. (*Moves forward to the barrel.*) Half two?

(*He steps back, deflated, and picks up the helmet. The two men circle him.*)

PORTER: (*Turning with a shrug of his shoulders*) Welcome home, Arthur!

(*As the two of them leave the stage the* FRIEND *has come around from the back of the stage carrying a mask in each hand. The* FRIEND *will speak for both masks, changing her voice slightly for each.* FIRST MASK *peers down as if from a balcony.*)

FIRST MASK: (*Raised*) Come 'ere.

SECOND MASK: (*Lowered*) What?

FIRST MASK: Come 'ere.

SECOND MASK: (*Raised*) What?

(*The* GIRL *appears and, walking across the stage, goes to sit on the platform which is centre-stage.*)

FIRST MASK: That's her there, Phyllis! Moved in with him bold as brass and his mother barely cold in the grave. The young ones now. Would you be up to them? Never had that class of yoke here before he came back.

SECOND MASK: Wild like the mother, Mrs Doyle. And sure what harm are they doing? Isn't it good to see somebody smiling in this place?

FIRST MASK: I don't know. A fool's paradise never lasts long. It's easy to smile without two children bawling, it's easy to smile when you don't have to sell your soul to that bastard every time an electricity bill comes in, or one of them gets sick. (*Stops and stares off to left with alarm in her voice.*) Is that Mr Deignan's car, Phyllis, there stopped at the lights?

SECOND MASK: No, that's just brown. His is shite-coloured.

FIRST MASK: Some days you'd be afraid to take the plug out of the sink in case his head would pop up. You know what Mrs Kennedy said to him: 'You're so famous round here, Mr Deignan,' she said, 'they'll have you in the Wax Works soon, only they won't need to make a model of you.'

SECOND MASK: Will you relax, Mrs Doyle, it's moving off. Lord, you're fierce jumpy. What you need now is a toy boy.

FIRST MASK: A toy boy? I'm lucky to get a bar of KitKat and a lie in. Come 'ere to me.

(*The masks are drawn closer and the voice drops.*)

Do you know what he said to me the other morning, the youngest crying in the next room and him lying there with the teeth in the glass beside the bed?

(*The* FRIEND *begins to lower the masks down.*)

He puts a hand out suddenly and, says he (*a gruff mumble*), 'Lie back, Rosie, it's Saturday.'
(*The lights go down and up on where* ARTHUR *is to the far left of the stage, staring into the wings as though gazing from window. The* GIRL *is behind him, lying on the platform.*)

ARTHUR: He's out there again.

GIRL: Who is?

ARTHUR: Deignan.

GIRL: Forget him.

ARTHUR: (*Bitterly*) God, I remember him now, a little brat in short trousers, perpetual snot on his nose and even then he could buy and sell you. He used to steal sweets from the mother and flog them for half-price. Then when we were fourteen . . . I remember . . . it was johnnies. Don't know where he got them, but he told the whole school I'd bought four off him one evening and came back the next day for two. Jaysus, they were buying them by the newtide, every penny they had . . . hidden under beds, going green, never used . . . and back next week for more in case he'd tell people they hadn't needed them.
(*The* GIRL *laughs.*)
Before I went away I saw him one night . . . Monkstown . . . all the little rich kids with money and no sense. He was selling them joints, ready-rolled for half a crown. They were having to be carried home to Mammy by their friends. I took the pull . . . herbal tobacco and loose shag . . . he winked up at me: 'Do you want a cut, Arthur, be my man here.' Christ, he looked pathetic, the elephant flares, huge tie like a red carpet. (*He pauses and his tone changes.*) I saw him yesterday in Drumcondra. Collecting rent. He's four houses there in flats. Warrens. You should have seen the number of bells on every door.

GIRL: Who gives a fuck about him? Come away, Arthur.

ARTHUR: That Doyle woman is with him. Like a dog keeping its distance, terrified of a kick.

GIRL: Arthur! You're like an old woman staring out that window. You get on my nerves whenever he's around.
(ARTHUR *turns.*)

49

ARTHUR: Have we tea?

GIRL: You know we haven't. We'll do without. It's not important.

ARTHUR: Dole day tomorrow.

GIRL: I know. It's OK.

ARTHUR: Bread?

GIRL: Arthur, stop this.

ARTHUR: It was easier by myself. I didn't mind the bad days.
Just take to the bed, take them in my stride. But now . . .

GIRL: Don't, Arthur, please.

ARTHUR: You know I'm trying, love. Every old foreman I
knew. Every factory that's left. I want to look after you.

GIRL: (*Screams*) Stop! Can't you see? You'll become like
them, you're sounding like my Da.
(*She rises as* ARTHUR *tries to speak.*)
I'm not fragile. I'm not some ornament made of glass. I'm
flesh and I'm blood and I don't need looking after – I
need to live. Listen, you're different, Arthur, and I don't
mind if we starve, just don't change, not for me.

ARTHUR: I just want to give you . . . things.

GIRL: I didn't come to you for things. I came to you for hope.
I can do without anything, except that. Shag the tea and
the bread, Arthur, just make me laugh.
(*He sits on the floor and looks up at her.*)

ARTHUR: The vegetarian that died . . .

GIRL: There was a big turnip at the funeral.
(*He claps his hands in a flourish. They both laugh.*)

ARTHUR: Did you hear about the blind circumciser?

GIRL: Don't tell me.

ARTHUR: He got the sack. (*Winces, then continues.*) Or the
Kerry suicide found hanging from the ceiling? What was
he called?

GIRL: What?

ARTHUR: Sean D'Olier.

GIRL: Where do you find them?

ARTHUR: Met them all on a bus last week, they were getting
the free travel. (*Pause.*) Maybe I've been away so long

they're new again. (*Pause.*) Some days I get lost. Do you know that? My feet think they know the way and I find myself turning down a side street that's gone. There's nothing there, just a few barrels and some old gotchie in a hut watching over the cars parked where the buildings used to be. Sometimes . . . it frightens me . . . you know like in a dream . . . the sequence doesn't make sense . . .

(*The* GIRL *climbs to her feet and interrupts him suddenly, blurting the sentence out, half embarrassed.*)

GIRL: I love you, Arthur. At first I wasn't sure. First I was just running away from everything else. But now I know. I'll follow you anywhere, any place. I want to live in that city you carry in your heart. You don't need this place to make it real, it's dead here, finished. We could go away, together. We could be free, Arthur. Out in those foreign cities you've talked about, those names . . .

ARTHUR: No. (*Shouts.*) Why do you always say this? Why can't you let me be . . . here?

GIRL: It's killing you. You're changing. Go, Arthur.

ARTHUR: No. I'm . . . (*Quietly*) I'm scared to go back. Fifteen years, love. In limbo – *Autobahns*, trains, borders. But I was never homeless, always knew I'd come back. Here, at least, I know who I am. I don't have to register my address with the police. Can't you see that, love? (*Glances towards the window again.*) He's back.

GIRL: Who?

ARTHUR: Deignan. With her again . . . that Doyle woman.

GIRL: Sure, it's only around the corner.

ARTHUR: What is?

GIRL: You don't know, Arthur, sure you don't. You don't know nothing. The post office, Arthur. It's children's allowance day. He holds her book as security, gives it to her before she goes in to collect, takes it and the cash from her when she comes out.

(ARTHUR *stares at her.*)

You just don't understand this city, do you?

(ARTHUR *is silent for a moment, taking this in.*)

ARTHUR: The bastard! I'll kill him!

(*He goes to move towards the door and the* GIRL *jumps up to grab him. She tries to calm him as he curses Deignan.*)

Little jumped-up bastard! I should have drowned him when I had the chance!

GIRL: For Christ's sake, Arthur, stop! Have sense!

(*They tussle, at first with him trying to break free and her attempting to restrain him but gradually the struggle turns into an embrace.*)

I don't want to lose you. Don't want to go back to that . . . hopelessness.

(*He strokes her hair, soothing her.*)

ARTHUR: There's nothing to fear, love. I've had his measure all my life.

GIRL: (*Softly*) Not any more, Arthur. He's more dangerous than you think. You don't know him. How he works.

ARTHUR: All my life I've known him and his sort.

GIRL: For my sake, fear him.

ARTHUR: You're always afraid.

GIRL: Afraid for you. For the rest, I would spit in their faces. It's so good here with you it frightens me. I keep saying that, I keep thinking nothing this good can last.

ARTHUR: (*Stroking her hair*) When I found you I found home again. No matter what you say. No matter if I get lost at times. With you, Kathy, it feels like it was. There's nothing more I want now, nowhere else to go. At times it's like this whole city's in terror of something that will never happen. Let's forget them all. We have this flat and each other, there's nobody can break that apart.

GIRL: (*Turning to look up at him with urgency in her voice*) Arthur, listen to me, they're all watching you and you don't realize it. The pushers, they hate the way you look at them. Even the kids round here, Arthur, they haven't a clue who you are. I see them dismantling that bike with their eyes, breaking it down into needles and fixes. To them all, you're just an outsider. And now Deignan. You remind him of things. His kind own this city now, Arthur. He'll want to own you as well. Don't you know that?

ARTHUR: (*Laughing as he climbs up on the platform*) I own this city and you and the thousands of us who live in warrens of estates and these blocks of crumbling flats. It's ours, Kathy, and it doesn't matter what titles they give themselves or what rackrents they collect, it doesn't even matter if they tear down every street so we can't recognize it. They still can't take it away from us. Because when they're rotting in the soil there'll still be thousands of us, swarming out into the thoroughfares every evening. (*Climbs down to take her in his arms.*) Come on, no more squabbling. This room is getting us down. (*Runs his hand down to her chin and gently cups it.*) Lift up your head, Kathy. We'll leave the bike here for a change, walk down through our town together, yours and mine. I want to show you off.

(*She looks up at him and they kiss.*)

GIRL: You never heard a word I said, did you?

ARTHUR: (*Smiles*) Silly talk from a silly time.

(*He begins to walk across the stage with her legs resting on his.*)

Dole day tomorrow, love. Bread, tea, pints of Guinness and, you'll see, work will come soon. Summer's coming. I could always knock out a living in the summer months, no matter what. Just wait. That's when it will all come back. Trust me.

(*Suddenly the* FRIEND *rushes on stage and barges against* ARTHUR's *back, separating them.* ARTHUR *looks back startled as the* FRIEND *vanishes. The* GIRL *has drifted from the stage. As we hear a shout off the stage from the* PORTER, ARTHUR *walks back to raise the platform again and begins to wipe his hands on a piece of cloth as if fixing his bike. The* PORTER *races on stage and runs to the far end. The* FRONTIER GUARD *follows him more slowly.*)

FRONTIER GUARD: (*Calling to the* PORTER) Don't bother your bollix, Pascal, you'll only be wasting your time there.

(*Catches his breath and points.*) Six hallways, two back entrances and twenty-four front doors. You might as well be pissing against the wind. We'll just wait here and watch.

(*The* PORTER *leans on the back wall and stares up.*)

PORTER: (*Breathless*) You wouldn't mind only they'll flog the stuff for a tenth of the price. (*Catches his breath.*) It's demoralizing this. I don't know, years ago you used to get to chase a much better class of criminal. I'm too old for this carry on.

(*The* FRONTIER GUARD *has walked over to the centre of the stage and spotted* ARTHUR. *He approaches him.*)

FRONTIER GUARD: Columbus was right, Pascal. The world is round and the same faces keep spinning back. You go and check the hallways.

PORTER: What's the point? You said yourself . . .

FRONTIER GUARD: Just do it!

PORTER: (*Resigned*) Right.

(*He exits and the* FRONTIER GUARD *approaches* ARTHUR *who has been ignoring them.*)

FRONTIER GUARD: Thought I'd seen the back of you, Cleary.

ARTHUR: Would be a foolish man to show his back to you, Mr Lynch.

FRONTIER GUARD: Detective Lynch to you. Always the bitter word. Like the mother. Sorry to hear about her, Arthur.

(*He pats* ARTHUR'*s shoulder.* ARTHUR *nods, accepting the condolence.*)

She was a good woman, always made me the cup of tea when I had to come and take you in. But sure, you were only children. God knows youse thought youse were the toughest men in the world, but you were like babes compared to the lads on the go now. Like babes in the wood, eh, Cleary?

ARTHUR: So you say, Mr Lynch.

FRONTIER GUARD: (*Putting his arm on* ARTHUR'*s shoulder*) You wouldn't be nervous now to be seen out here talking to me, Cleary?

ARTHUR: You know me, Mr Lynch, I'd talk to the dog in the street.

FRONTIER GUARD: (*Looking up at the mass of windows above*) But nobody else knows you, Cleary. You should be nervous. They're watching us from up there. They're wondering.

ARTHUR: Shag them.

FRONTIER GUARD: It's them shagging you I'd be more worried about. (*Walks back to* ARTHUR *and changes tone.*) I think you've a problem, Cleary.

ARTHUR: I'm listening.

FRONTIER GUARD: A problem of perspective. Where do you stand now? This isn't the messing you and your friends got up to. This isn't a crate of beer fecked off a lorry, or a fist fight in a lousy cinema. There is a woman back there lying in a pool of her own blood – they went for her handbag and took half her arm. There is an old man down there at the traffic lights with a piece of glass stuck in his eyes where the bastards broke the window of his car. That was never your scene, Arthur. I know you since you were mitching from school. Are you with them, Cleary, or are you with me?

(ARTHUR *turns to look at him for the first time.*)

ARTHUR: You always took your work fierce personal, Mr Lynch. You don't give a shite if that man loses his sight. I remember you chasing me after that fight outside the Savoy. Two nights you spent sitting in the wasteground across there, waiting for me to come home for a meal. It's still your private game isn't it, you alone against them? You're a bit old for this, Mr Lynch. Have they no desk jobs?

(*The* FRONTIER GUARD *spits.*)

FRONTIER GUARD: Ah fuck their desks and their computers. You don't fight these bastards on a screen. I'm not ready for grass yet. Listen, Arthur, you'll need me yet. I've ears you know and you've got an acute shortage of friends in this neighbourhood.

ARTHUR: I'll take my chances.

FRONTIER GUARD: Come on, Arthur, pick a side. I could use a pair of eyes, Arthur, and you could use a friend.

ARTHUR: You were always good at using.

FRONTIER GUARD: (*Angry*) You saw a girl come in here. Don't tell us you didn't.

PORTER: (*Shouts from off-stage*) Nothing out here!

ARTHUR: Your little friend might need help by now, or do you not fancy the tricky corners any more?

FRONTIER GUARD: (*Shouts*) Pascal, get out here. (*Threateningly to* ARTHUR) I asked you a question.

ARTHUR: What girl?

(*The* PORTER *returns, slightly out of breath. We understand that he does not know* ARTHUR *and presumes there is a standard questioning of a suspect taking place.*)

FRONTIER GUARD: You were messing with that bike like you're always doing. Now don't tell me you didn't see a girl.

(*No response.*)

(*Shouts*) I'm talking to you, sonny!

ARTHUR: (*Looking up*) Daddy?

FRONTIER GUARD: Don't get fresh with me. Just don't. I don't know what you're doing back here, but I know it's illegal. It has to be, you look fucking happy.

PORTER: (*Circling* ARTHUR) Is that your bike, Cleary?

ARTHUR: Yeah.

PORTER: (*Circling* ARTHUR) Have you the tax up to date on that?

ARTHUR: Yes.

PORTER: Insurance?

ARTHUR: Yeah.

PORTER: (*Miming speaking into a radio with his back to the audience*) What's the registration number?

ARTHUR: PSI 850.

FRONTIER GUARD: One of these times I'm taking you down for a nostalgic visit to the station. How'd you fancy a surgical glove up the arse?

ARTHUR: (*Quietly*) Cost me fifty guilders in any other country.

FRONTIER GUARD: You've made your choice, Cleary. Now you can sink or swim in it. Do you get my drift?

ARTHUR: Yes, Mr Lynch, and I know you're really saying, welcome home, son.

(*Lights go down again on centre of stage and rise on the* GIRL *who walks on from the right.*)

GIRL: Grief is a knot
That is choking my throat
Rage is a whirlwind
Imploding through my skull

If only I had known
Your life to be in danger
I would have clawed
My way between you and them

I would have bitten
Into their skin with my teeth
I would have stubbed
Out their eyes with my nails

If only I had shouted
When you walked from the flat
Or ran to the balcony
Still naked to call you back

(*The* FRONTIER GUARD *has retreated behind the raised platform with a mask over his face. The* PORTER *approaches him from the left and mimes handing something to him as music begins to intrude on the verses. He receives in return a bag of white powder. The* FRIEND *has approached from the left. The following muffled dialogue takes place in the background while the* GIRL *is still reciting.*)

FRONTIER GUARD: What do you want?

FRIEND: I need some stuff.

FRONTIER GUARD: Where's the money? Where's the money?

FRIEND: I'll get it tomorrow.

(*The* FRONTIER GUARD *gestures with his hand and then vanishes. The* GIRL *finishes reciting and remains to the left of the stage. The* FRIEND *is pulling at the platform and shouting over the loud music.*)

I'll get you the money! I'll get you the money! I'll get you the money tomorrow.

(*She pushes the platform and as it falls the entire stage goes black. The frontier-post music begins and the* PORTER, *now lying under the platform that* ARTHUR *is standing on, begins to shine the light up and down through the bars. The* FRONTIER GUARD *enters and shines the torch directly into* ARTHUR's *face.*)

FRONTIER GUARD: Passport, please.

(ARTHUR *turns.*)

ARTHUR: Sorry.

(*Hands him the passport which the* FRONTIER GUARD *opens and examines.*)

FRONTIER GUARD: Ah Irish. Irish. Boom-boom! Eh!

(*He laughs.*)

ARTHUR: I know that joke. You've made that before. It's . . . it's like a dream . . . recurring. I know you. Where is this place, what side of the border am I on?

FRONTIER GUARD: What does it matter to you, Irish? Either side you're a long way from home.

ARTHUR: (*Shrugs his head towards window*) What's he looking at the wheels for?

FRONTIER GUARD: Looking for? It's the rules, Irish, the rules.

(*He hands back the passport and turns to stare out towards the right of the stage.*)

ARTHUR: Wait!

(*The* FRONTIER GUARD *stops with his back turned.*)

How long have we been here?

(*No reply.*)

I keep thinking this . . . happened before. I can't remember things like I used to. Have I shown you my passport already?

(*He waits but no reply.*)

Turn around. I know your face. I have seen you before.
Why are we so long here? Tell me! (*Raises voice.*) What's
keeping us here?

FRONTIER GUARD: (*Turning sharply and blinding* ARTHUR
with the torch) You are keeping us here.

(*The* FRONTIER GUARD *turns away again.*)

ARTHUR: What do you mean? That doesn't make sense.
(*Shouts.*) What country have I come from? I can't remember! I can't! Which one?

FRONTIER GUARD: One you cannot return to.

ARTHUR: Why? What have I done? Had I an accident? Why
can't I remember anything? How do I know your face?

(*The* FRONTIER GUARD *begins to move.*)

No, wait! I'm talking to you!

(*The* FRONTIER GUARD *steps out of the light and walks to
the left of stage.* ARTHUR *stares after him, then turns to
shout under the platform.*)

Hey! You! Where is this place?

(*The* PORTER, *without acknowledging his presence, switches
the torch off and, crawling out, moves to left of stage where
the* FRIEND *is now standing.*)

Where . . . ?

(*The* FRONTIER GUARD *walks up to the* GIRL *as if to a
widow at a wake.*)

FRONTIER GUARD: You know, he was a legend . . .

(ARTHUR *is left alone standing on top of the platform.*)

ARTHUR: It was clear until I started thinking about it. Like
I've been here for ever waiting for this train to start . . .

FRONTIER GUARD: I used to look up to him in school. You
know, I could have been a help to him settling in.

(*He walks away from her.*)

ARTHUR: Can't . . . it's all fading. Wait. A laneway . . . that's
right, flowers between the stones . . . barbed wire . . . bits
of glass . . .

GIRL: (*Cries*) Arthur!

ARTHUR: And a girl! That's right, no name, can't remember,
too painful . . . I loved her, she was younger, Dublin . . .

FRIEND: Wild, like his mother, that lad.

ARTHUR: But why was I running . . . suddenly scared?

FRIEND: The door was open day and night, children sleeping on the floor whenever their mothers were in hospital. As poor as anyone here herself but she always gave.

(ARTHUR *clutches the belt he is wearing then lifts his hands up in shock.*)

ARTHUR: My belt, it's begun to rot. Like it were transformed back into flesh.

FRIEND: Never begrudged him, but the life was gone from her.

ARTHUR: How long? I must remember. A laneway, then what? A journey through empty streets.

FRIEND: The lad should have watched his step.

(*The* FRIEND *retreats and the* PORTER *approaches the* GIRL.)

ARTHUR: Night time . . . walking for hours. From the laneway. Why? I was going somewhere, but couldn't leave.

PORTER: The real McCoy, Arthur Cleary.

ARTHUR: Cars abandoned, bronze statues in O'Connell Street staring down.

PORTER: Always drifting from one job to the next.

ARTHUR: Where has everyone gone? Only one voice like a whisper from a side street . . . calling me back . . .

GIRL: (*Cries*) Arthur!

(*The* PORTER *retreats from her.*)

ARTHUR: Not letting me go. Had to find her . . . The night went black, the moon dim like the end of a tunnel. I'm swimming towards it, but . . . always pulled back . . . by her voice, calling. And then . . . here . . . why? Why?

GIRL: (*Screams*) Arthur!

(*She shudders as if coming out of a dream and looks over to where* ARTHUR *is standing on the platform.*)

You weren't there when I woke. I was frightened.

(*She walks towards him and he embraces her, soothing her as he strokes her hair and they sit on the edge of the platform.*)

ARTHUR: (*Soothing*) Frightened? Of what?

GIRL: Arthur ... (*Pause.*) Tell me about it all again, where you fed the swans on the steps on a Sunday. All the places. The sounds of the names are lovely, like ... like legends, dreams. I can see it when you talk.

ARTHUR: (*Teasing softly*) Capel Street, Rialto, Phibsborough ...

GIRL: No, Arthur, say them. They're far away, safe.

ARTHUR: (*Quietly, soothing*) Altona. Blankensee, with little cobbled steps and terrace cafés built on jetties on to the Elbe that would rock in the wake of the boats passing. Wedel where the ships would play their national anthems as they left the mouth of the river.

GIRL: Wedel.

ARTHUR: And the dormitories. Always the same. That time my ribs were cracked in the strike of foreign pickers and I lay for a week in the third bunk up, staring at the streets of Dublin tattooed along the veins of my wrist. The stink of Turkish cigarettes, photos of kids, pin-ups, and always at night the same talk of returning, even if you couldn't follow the languages, you knew what they were talking about.

GIRL: And then you came back. You never told me why, Arthur.

(*Pause.*)

ARTHUR: Can't really explain it. Just happened one night, halted at a border post. Lines of tracks, containers stacked on sidings. I'd pulled the window down to watch a guard shining his light under the train when suddenly I was overcome with a longing for something ... I don't know ... something I'd lost ... (*Pause.*) I keep thinking I've found it and it slips away again.

GIRL: A city's like a person, Arthur, it can never stay the same.

ARTHUR: In that limbo between states I wanted it back, everything ... waking in the bay windows of flats with a raw throat from drink, walking to the Fifteen Acres for a game of ball, or back along the quays always bumping into

someone. Even when you were broke you felt you belonged.
Never felt that way anywhere else.

GIRL: Arthur, we could try . . . there's England . . .

(*He pauses as if trying to understand it himself as well as tell
her.*)

ARTHUR: (*Quietly*) Could have been that way for ever, drifting
from city to city. Only something happened at that border
post. I saw my reflection in the window . . . so suddenly
old, so stale with experience. I felt this panic I couldn't
explain . . . that if I stayed in the carriage I would be
damned to wander for ever across that continent. The
guard had stamped my passport and made the usual joke.
I was alone. I turned the door handle and jumped, began
to run as the official with the torch shouted after me. I
never looked back, just dodged past shunting wagons and
containers till I reached the gates and was out into the
countryside. There was woodland, through the foliage I
could see lights of trucks from an *Autobahn*. I kept running
until I came to what I thought was a ruined house. When
I got closer I realized it was a war monument, the shell of
a building where people had been shot. I smoked cigarettes
all night leaning against the plaque, clutching that battered
green passport in my hands. Next morning I hitched to
the nearest port, caught a ferry to Holland, a plane from
there. Ireland's Eye, Lambay, wheeling over Swords so
huge below me it was hard to believe I was home.

(*On the word 'home' there is a loud banging as the* FRON-
TIER GUARD *slaps his money-lender's book against the
wooden support on the right of the stage.* ARTHUR *and the*
GIRL *part and rise. They stand as if in a doorway, facing
away from the* FRONTIER GUARD.)

FRONTIER GUARD: (*In Deignan voice*) Mrs Doyle, this is
ridiculous. I am not blind or stupid. I know you are in
there. You've had enough warnings already. I'll smash
this door down if I have to! Do you hear?

(*The* FRONTIER GUARD *sees* ARTHUR *and stares at him.*)
Still here, Arthur.

(*No reply.*)

Hear you haven't been too lucky on the job front. It's a tough one.

ARTHUR: (*Turning*) Summer's coming, Deignan.

FRONTIER GUARD: So is Christmas. Listen to me, Arthur, I don't like to see a school pal down on his luck. I've a lot of business in this block, but it's troublesome, a lot of hassle. Time is money, you know what I mean. I'm too busy to chase it. I could use somebody, someone I could trust, to keep an eye on things for me.

ARTHUR: Summer's coming, I'll be busy.

FRONTIER GUARD: Doing what? Mugging tourists? Cleaning kitchens at two pounds an hour? Listen. I'm not talking anything heavy, Arthur, and the money'd be good. Right, you've a few messers like the Doyles, but the rest are no problem. I mean . . . they're grateful. Genuine. Ask yourself what bank wants to know people here? If it wasn't for me, Arthur . . . there'd be nothing bought . . . no furniture, no clothes at communion time, no presents at Christmas, ESB cutting people off. We're talking about people nobody else gives a shite about, we're talking about providing a service . . .

ARTHUR: (*Cutting in firmly*) Thanks anyway.

FRONTIER GUARD: (*Sharper*) Think about it, Cleary. You'll be a long time rotting in that flat. It's the best offer you're likely to get.

ARTHUR: I'll manage.

FRONTIER GUARD: OK, suit yourself.

(*He turns to walk off and has gone a few paces before he turns back. His tone changes slightly.*)

Well, just do this for me so. (*Opening book*) When you see Mrs Doyle, you tell her from me . . .

ARTHUR: Do your own dirty work, Deignan.

FRONTIER GUARD: (*Sinister tone*) I don't think you realize the situation here, Cleary. This is now, it's not your mother running up and down here telling people what they're entitled to. You think you're somebody, Cleary, because you swaggered around here once. I'm not asking you, I'm telling . . .

(ARTHUR *moves forward as the* GIRL *grabs his shoulder to try to hold him back.*)

GIRL: No Arthur, no . . .

ARTHUR: (*Shouts*) The scum of the fucking earth. You weren't born, Deignan, your mother hatched you out in the back of that filthy shop! You and that spa of a brother of yours!

FRONTIER GUARD: It wasn't your money made my family rich, with your twist of tea and your Vincent de Paul vouchers!

(ARTHUR *grabs the folder from the* FRONTIER GUARD'*s hands. He releases the clip, turns, and throws the papers up in the air, scattering the pages down into the audience as if over a balcony into a courtyard.*)

GIRL: Oh Jesus! No! Oh God!

FRONTIER GUARD: (*Shaken but in a low voice*) You pick up every one of those, Cleary.

GIRL: (*Terrified*) I'll go, I will . . .

(*She moves to brush past* ARTHUR, *who stops her with his hand and reaches out with his right to grip the* FRONTIER GUARD'*s shirt and pull him towards him.*)

ARTHUR: (*Quietly but with menace*) Don't ever address me again, Deignan. Don't ever come near me, don't even be on the same landing as me. Ever.

(*The* FRONTIER GUARD *squares up to* ARTHUR *as if about to strike him, but suddenly flinches when* ARTHUR *blows into his face.* ARTHUR *releases him dismissively.*)

FRONTIER GUARD: You're a posthumous man, Cleary. Do you hear me? I don't strike the dead, it's not worth the effort.

(*The* FRONTIER GUARD *backs off-stage. The* GIRL *is gazing down into the audience at the pages.*)

GIRL: (*Softly as she reaches her arms out as though trying to catch the papers*) Blowing, like death warrants, death warrants.

(*The* GIRL *moves to stand against the backdrop of the stage.*

As she speaks she tears at the cloth with her hands and it comes away leaving a blood-red background. Music begins.)

GIRL'S VOICE: (*Recorded*)

You went down steps
Because the lift was broken
You paused outside
And strolled out of my life

Across a courtyard
Where housewives were talking
Lying between sheets
I could hear the engine start

(*As she has been reciting, the masked figures of the* FRIEND, *the* PORTER *and the* FRONTIER GUARD *have begun to close in on* ARTHUR *from the back of the stage with raised sticks in their hands. The* PORTER *is laughing, a hollow, mocking sound.*)

GIRL: I drifted into sleep
To see a horse come riderless
Over fields trailing
A bridle smeared with blood

Towards a white house
Where a woman stood screaming
As I shuddered awake
I realized her voice was mine.

(*All light has died except for one flashing white light shining from the front of the audience.* ARTHUR *runs to his right where the* FRONTIER GUARD *kicks the barrel towards him.* ARTHUR *catches it, falling backwards and throws it himself so that he lands with the barrel like a pillow behind him. Over the intense music the* PORTER *strikes the barrel a number of times as the others raise their sticks.* ARTHUR *shudders each time the barrel is struck and then hangs limply against it as the scene dissolves into a sudden blackout. The* PORTER *and* FRIEND *in blackout switch on torches which flicker over the dead body of* CLEARY *and then out to play over the faces of the audience. The* FRONTIER GUARD *is lowering the platform and* CLEARY *rises to sit on one edge of it with the* FRONTIER GUARD *sitting down on the other. The two torches swing around so that both figures are caught within a separate beam of light.*)

FRONTIER GUARD: (*Speaking as if just going through the motions*) Passport, please.

(ARTHUR *turns.*)

ARTHUR: Sorry.

(*He doesn't hand over the passport but the* FRONTIER GUARD *still speaks.*)

FRONTIER GUARD: Ah Irish. Boom-boom! Eh!

(*He laughs.*)

ARTHUR: I know that joke. You've made that before. I . . . I know you. Where's this place, which side . . .

(*His voice trails off in sudden fear.*)

FRONTIER GUARD: (*Interrupting*) What difference does it make? Either side you're a long way from home.

ARTHUR: (*Speaking as though going through the motions of a dream*) What's he . . . ?

FRONTIER GUARD: Looking for? It's the rules, Irish.

ARTHUR: I have shown you my passport already. I have been here before.

(*Slight pause.*)

FRONTIER GUARD: Yes.

ARTHUR: (*Quieter*) Then why are we stopped?

FRONTIER GUARD: It is the border, Irish.

ARTHUR: Which border? Where am I?

FRONTIER GUARD: Don't you know by now?

ARTHUR: (*Thinks; then quietly*) This is it, isn't it? This is as far as you take me?

FRONTIER GUARD: You catch on faster than most.

ARTHUR: How long . . . do we wait here?

FRONTIER GUARD: Till you decide to go.

ARTHUR: It's funny ... so much I can remember now. (*Pauses.*) Her name, the feel of her skin. She was younger, you know, far younger than me.

FRONTIER GUARD: She was then.

ARTHUR: What do you mean?

FRONTIER GUARD: So many trains run through here, day and night, in all directions, all times, coming and going.

ARTHUR: (*Looking down at platform*) Who's on that one? Where's it going?

FRONTIER GUARD: Europe ... The future ... Her children.

ARTHUR: Not mine.

FRONTIER GUARD: (*Smiles*) Life goes on, you pick the pieces up. Would you have had her put on black and spin out her life in mourning?

ARTHUR: Do they know of me? These children?

FRONTIER GUARD: She taught them your name like a secret tongue.

ARTHUR: It goes on so ... without me.

FRONTIER GUARD: She cried, Cleary, walking the quays, praying for the courage to hurl herself in. She held you here for years, begging you to haunt her. Then she learnt to let you go, so you could pass on, not remain trapped in her grief.

ARTHUR: Then why am I still here?

FRONTIER GUARD: You must let her go, not plague her dreams.

ARTHUR: How?

FRONTIER GUARD: I'm only the railway guard, Irish.

(*There is silence for a moment.*)

Forget them, Irish, forget her. This is between you ...

(ARTHUR *slowly turns to the waiting guard.*)

ARTHUR: And who?

(*There is no reply.*)

What's out there in front of me?

(*The* FRONTIER GUARD *shrugs his shoulders.*)

I have your face now. You've been with me all along, haven't you?

(*There is no reply.* ARTHUR *waits a moment before continuing.*)

What do I have to do?

FRONTIER GUARD: Remember everything, every moment, longing, whisper, every touch you've ever known.

ARTHUR: And then?

FRONTIER GUARD: Let go.

(*The torch light on the* FRONTIER GUARD *goes out suddenly.*)

ARTHUR: Into nothing? Is there any . . . ?

(*He waits for assurance. The* FRONTIER GUARD *offers none.*)

I was always clinging on. Never able to change. (*Silence.*) It's not easy. I'm scared. (*Half-laugh.*) All so suddenly precious. Every moment like a film running through my skull. Never wanted it back so badly.

(*He looks slowly around him, wipes his lips nervously and then stares down at his hands for a moment, before raising them slightly.*)

Let go.

(*The torch light on him, dies on the word 'go'. The stage is left in total darkness and briefly over the faint music we hear the sound of train wheels growing in volume for a few moments before fading away.*)

THE TRAMWAY END

In High Germany

'Thoughtful, comic, sad and provocative, this monologue of a lost and altered heritage is vigorously and intelligently played by Stephen Brennan . . . These two plays (*The Tramway End*) are cogent manifestations of a changing Irish world and, for that alone, and more, are well worth seeing.'

Irish Times

'Serious, interesting writing from Bolger, it speaks at the very least for the generation reared in the sixties and gives voice to some timely questions about our view of ourselves.'

Sunday Tribune

'*In High Germany* is important for its recognition of the unifying role that soccer plays in the great Irish *diaspora*. The theme is portrayed superbly by Stephen Brennan from the compelling vantage point of a German railway station.'

Sunday Press

In High Germany is a one-act play for one character, EOIN.

The action takes place on platform 4 of Altona railway station, Hamburg, Germany. The time is just after midnight on 19 June 1988.

In High Germany was first staged by the Gate Theatre, Dublin, as part of the Dublin Theatre Festival on 9 October 1990. The role of EOIN was played by Stephen Brennan. It was staged as part of *The Tramway End* – along with *The Holy Ground* – with a new design by Robert Ballagh on 9 November 1990. The design used in the text is by Robert Ballagh.

Director	David Byrne
Designer	Ned McLoughlin
Lighting Designer	Conleth White
Production Manager	Rupert Murray
Stage Director	Michael Higgins
ASM	Millie Magnier

The stage begins in darkness with the crackle of a loudspeaker announcing in German the arrival of a train from Essen to Hamburg, Altona. As the play progresses there will occasionally be another distant announcement or the rumble of a train far off. The backdrop of the stage is curved like the wall of a U-bahn platform, and its harsh whiteness is broken by the glaring colour of a series of advertisements in German with a white light above each. There are two poles, one at the centre right of the stage and one at the centre left, with three plastic chairs attached to each. A sign high on the wall reads 'HAMBURG, Altona', and further back a station clock shows that the time is ten past one in the morning. A shutter sign suspended at one end of the platform flaps down until it is blank to indicate that the final train has gone. On the right is an Ausgang *sign for the exit and on the left an* Eingang *sign for the entrance.* EOIN *walks silently on from the left and, throwing his bag and sleeping bag (which are tied together) down beside the pole on the right, stares at a piece of paper furled into a ball in the centre of the stage. He is in his early thirties, wearing jeans and a leather jacket with a 1980s Ireland soccer jersey on him and an Ireland scarf around his neck. He walks back towards the side wall where the* Eingang *sign is and taps his hands on it, beginning to beat louder with the growing chant.*

EOIN: Ireland! Ireland! Ireland! Ireland!

The chant and banging reach a crescendo and he stops suddenly and turns around, walking back towards the paper and giving it a

75

few kicks around the stage. He is muttering to himself in a country accent.

Solo it, solo it, solo it . . .

He kicks the paper ball across the stage and turns, speaking the first sentence almost to himself as he unwraps the scarf from his neck.

If only we could have clung on . . . (*Pause.*) The road from the stadium was paved with stones. Real ones, I mean, thousands of them littered on the ground. Almost as many stones as Dutch supporters. Thought about those stones a lot this afternoon in that stadium when I could think anything, sweating with the heat, sweating with the fear, throat raw from shouting, hands raised . . .

He lifts the scarf suddenly in the air and chants:

Ireland! Ireland! Ireland!

He lowers the scarf again, brought back to earth.

How would we get out of that stadium alive, down that half-mile of loose stones and away from the Dutch fans if Ireland clung on for a draw? But really I didn't give a shite how we'd get down it. I'd have faced any barrage of rocks if we could cling on, carry on to Hamburg (*Looks up*) if I could carry on back to here, not alone but as still part of . . .

He walks over to his bag and, sitting down, puts the scarf into the bag. He looks up.

In Gelsenkirchen this afternoon they had these little scuttery trains . . . like underground trams . . . only room for maybe forty people squeezed up.

He rises.

We boarded one, up in the concrete plaza where we'd been drinking the local beer, around fifty of us, packed in, and took off for the stadium. The first stop was grand, no one on, no one off. The second stop was the problem. There was about sixty of them . . . Dutch skinheads . . . the real McCoy – not the fey little farts of students we'd seen in Amsterdam, all Auschwitz pyjamas and haircuts to cure headlice – these boys were mean bastards. Shaven heads painted orange, boots thicker than the walls of Limerick jail, sticks in their hands, eyes like boiled sweets from Bray that would break your teeth.

They didn't all pack on – just as many as would fit between us and the roof. One of them had his face pressed against mine. I could smell the drink as I looked at him and swallowed, then . . .

He lifts his fist.

. . . did what every decent Irishman does when in doubt abroad . . . raised my fist in the air and slagged the Brits.

He thumps his fist off an imaginary ceiling and sings:

'If you hate the Queen of England clap your hands,
If you hate the Queen of England clap your hands . . .'

He lowers his fist and looks at audience.

The fuckers smiled, banged their sticks against the ceiling and sang. Would we ever get to that shagging stadium? The train stopping and starting, nobody getting on or off, every Irishman racking his brains.

He raises fist and sings frantically:

'Adversane England, Adversane England,
Adversane, Adversane, Adversane England . . .'

He circles the space where the Dutch skinhead would be and hisses urgently:

77

Smile, you shagging Dutch bastards, smile.

He sings:

'Robinson's mother is a man, do-da, do-da . . .'

Dutch accent:

'Ya, dodadoda!'

He presses himself up as though squeezed against somebody.

The Dutch skinner pressed against me produces a roll-up and gestures with his hand.

He raises two fingers to his lips and shouts:

'Fur!' I didn't need Shane to translate that. I reached in, took a lighter from my pocket and began to raise it.

He reaches into his pocket and takes out a lighter, which he holds up. We cannot see if there is anything printed on it or not.

Then I remembered. I'd two lighters. A plain white one and one I'd picked up in some bar in Stuttgart . . . embossed with a Union Jack. I closed my eyes, held it up and flicked it.

He holds his head sideways, grimacing in expectation of the blow as he flicks. He waits a second before cautiously opening his eyes and glancing at the lighter in his hand.

No thump came. I opened my eyes, the lighter was virginal white. And they say there's no God, eh?

He puts the light back in his pocket and walks backwards.

Trains . . . I've always had this dream about making a film set in a railway station. It has this secret agent, I don't know, Bulgarian or Russian or some crack like that.

He moves forward, outlining the blurred outline of tracks with his hands.

Anyway the film opens with him going to a deserted flat in Berlin to photograph secret documents when he gets hit over the skull and the screen plunges into blackness followed by this blurred succession of railway tracks, until suddenly he wakes up.

He looks up questioningly at the audience.

OK, he knows he's in a railway-station waiting room. But where? That's the question. There's just total silence, nobody about, the first glow of dawn at the grimy window above the wooden bench. Could it be France? Austria? The Transvaal? Nagorno-Karabakh? Armed guards outside, secret police, trumpet-wielding shepherds?

He lifts an imaginary fur coat to look.

A dead blonde on the platform, naked except for a fur coat and a tattoo of Lenin on her left buttock?

He jumps up on the left-hand-side seats and mimes throwing two windows open.

He mounts the bench, throws the window open, thrusts his head out and sees them . . . (*Pause.*) Sheep! Nothing but sheep! Thousands of the shaggers! The camera pans back to take in the sign over his head for . . .

He jumps down and, looking back, then gestures with his hands.

. . . Limerick Junction! (*Laughs.*) Limerick Junction, eh? That's how I always saw them, train stations. Victorian relics tucked away at the arse end of small towns. One train in the morning, one at night. Miss it and you were fucked. And, don't ask me how, but even if you were only going from Dublin to Drogheda you still always wound up sitting on your arse for two hours in Limerick Junction.

He sits down, remembering.

We saw them all on Sunday mornings when I was growing up. On our way to Turners Cross, Flower Lodge, Oriel Park, the Market's Field, Lourdes Stadium (*Blesses himself*) St Mel's Park. Once after Waterford beat Bohs the team bus broke down and the whole team had to come back with us.

Supporter's voice:

'What are you doing here?' one of the fans shouted at the manager in the queue.

Deeper voice:

'I'm getting a train ticket for the team.'

Supporter's voice:

'Jaysus, you'll be doing well. They aren't worth one!'

He rises and shuffles across the stage, scratching his arse as he waves an imaginary flag and speaks in his own voice.

Every station the same. Sleepy officials in oversized hats reluctantly shuffling out with a flag to wave the train on. And always the rusting metal bridge . . .

He stops and outlines its shape with his hands.

80

. . . the place-name laid out in white stones in a flower bed centuries ago and the platform like a ghost town until ten minutes before the train was due. We'd hang around the platform, Bohs scarfs around our necks, watching the little Civil Servants and Library Assistants being shunted back to bedsit-land by Mammy and Daddy, clean underwear in their bags.

Not that we always had it so easy, mind you. Limerick was a hole, Athlone the same. Every local thug and headbanger convinced they had to prove they were as tough as their brothers in the metropolis by kicking your head in.

Shane's accent:

'Welcome to Ireland . . .'

His own voice:

. . . Shane used to say, as we pissed down back lanes for our lives.

Shane's accent:

'They're just letting us know we're welcome!'

He leans against the wall at the right of the stage and speaks in his own voice.

It's funny, I suppose, the way train stations always fascinate me. Don't know . . . maybe it comes down to the old photos. My mother had stacks of them in an old biscuit tin under the sideboard. Meeting Daddy off the train at Westland Row, seeing Daddy back on to the train at Westland Row. How many times were strangers prevailed upon to snap them standing there, awkward together in public like any Irish married couple, a little space left for decency between them? That little space shrank and grew in Westland Row, the train wheels coming and going, chanting over and over . . .

He clenches his fist and moves his elbow like a piston.

You'll never go back! You'll never go back!

He walks over to sit down beside his bag and, opening it, begins to root inside for cigarettes, finally producing a packet of twenty.

Black '57. (*Pause.*) '57 was when the building game collapsed. I was one, a scuttery-arsed bundle of love. Daddy was a shadow coming and going from London, Birmingham, Coventry, a succession of registered letters with crisp English banknotes, a black travel-light bag carried in and out of Westland Row. Bottles of Guinness and Babycham for my mother the night before he'd go back and always the same song – 'And still I live in hopes to see, The Holy Ground once more'.

He takes the wrapping off the packet, takes out a cigarette and puts the packet back in the bag.

It would have been so much easier for him, I know, to have just picked up his one-year-old bundle and departed to a new life through Westland Row, like all his brothers and sisters had, but he refused to. He had guts, my Da, I'd say that for him. Guts and dreams.

He rises and walks over towards left-hand-side seats.

Dreams that I'd grow up under an Irish flag, knowing I belonged somewhere, a free person in a free land. (*Smiles ironically.*) Not that he'd have said it that way, or any way for that matter. Didn't speak much, my Da, just worked till he dropped a few weeks after the Yanks gave him the brush-off.

A pause as he lights the cigarette and inhales.

Their stories were like the best old films. They began and

ended in railway stations. So does this one, I suppose, for Mick and Shane and me. Real stations this time, or at least big stations, Hamburg and Essen. Hamburg in hope, Essen (*Thinks*) in farewell. (*Laughs quietly.*) Not places we ever dreamt we'd wind up in when we first met, Mick and Shane and me, all five years of age, short trousers, off to school, pissing ourselves with fright. I think Mick spoke first when we were seven. It was the first time Shane paused for breath. Scrawny, Shane was, and short, about the same centre of gravity as a duck . . .

He throws a footballing shape.

. . . lunging in after the ball, getting more kicks off other people than he ever got at it. Captain Shane, we called him.

Childish voice:

'Captain Shane Birdseye and his cod pieces.'

His own voice:

Took me eleven years to get the joke. Mick said he figured it out when he was six; he just didn't get around to laughing. Never got around to saying anything.

He jumps up on the seats and raises his fist in the air as though clutching a whip.

Molloy could ask him a question, hop up on the desk in full bondage gear, canes, whips, daggers, and Mick would just look at him with a complete moronic stare.

His face turns moronic as he lowers his arm.

Molloy never touched him. He'd turn away, defeated, snort some remark about planting Mick with the other vegetables in the fields and, as soon as his back was turned, without even looking down or changing expression, Mick would write the answer down on my copy book beside him.

He jumps down and looks around him.

Jesus, how could I even describe that school yard now? Like a scene from centuries ago. Acres of concrete split by weeds (*Fans his hands out slowly*), famished gulls wheeling overhead as we were herded into line . . .

He stands to attention and lifts his hands up and down in a straight line, taking on teacher's country voice:

'Suas, seas, suas, seas.'

He lowers his hands and uses them to describe the images he is describing.

Molloy, that rancid old bastard with his strap. And a bench like this . . . All the way down the concrete shed where we sat, talking, joking, laughing, eating lunch quickly . . . waiting to get out there . . . on the concrete . . . among the littered bread and papers . . . sandals, boots, shoes, runners scrambling, kicking out, rushing after a single dirty plastic ball. Forty forwards with no backs or keepers . . . coats piled up as goalposts . . . and there we'd be, Shane and Mick and me . . .

He mimes charging a ball, throwing himself into the air to head it.

. . . in the thick of it; kicking, shoving, scrambling, together, united, till we were caught.

He slowly draws himself to attention and stares straight ahead, lifting and dropping his hands, and speaks in master's voice:

'Suas, seas . . . suas, seas . . .'

He flinches slightly, as if expecting a blow, and speaks in own voice:

Touch the shoulder of the boy in front, look at his clipped hair, watch out for Molloy pacing behind ... Your legs still tingling, breath still heavy from that illicit game, feet itching for the last, the perfect kick, the cup-winning goal for Bohs.

He breaks rank as he is speaking and goes to kick an imaginary ball, freezing himself in the stance of kicking it. He stands back and points at the spot, speaking in the master's voice:

'This is a ball! A what, boy?'

Own boy's voice:

'A ball, sir.'

Master's voice:

'*As Gaelige!*'

Own boy's voice:

'*Liarod, a mhaister.*'

Master's voice:

'And what do you do with it, boy?'

Own boy's voice:

'Kick it, sir.'

Master's voice:

'And what else, boy?'

Own boy's voice but uncertain:

'Head it, sir?'

Master's voice, roaring:

'Pick it up! Pick it up! Pick it up! Pick it up!'

EOIN *stops in fear and mimes grabbing the ball up. Master's voice in staccato roar:*

'Not off the ground! Use your foot, use your foot off the ground! Solo it! Solo it! Solo it! Solo it!'

EOIN *miming awkwardly trying to run, solo-ing the ball, but loses control and drops it. Master's voice, infuriated:*

'What arse end of the bog did you come from at all, boy?'

His own voice:

'The street, sir, the city street.'

He sits down on the left-hand-side seats.

Had a slight cultural difficulty with me and Mick and Shane, Molloy did. The old bastard couldn't accept that we existed. Whatever the role-models were in his teacher training book they didn't include us . . . or streets or soccer.

He rises, impersonating the master.

'A Brit sport, an English sport played by Englishmen.'

He drops the cigarette on the ground, smiles and stubs it out.

I wish you'd lived to see Stuttgart, you old bastard.

He leans against the left-hand-side wall.

Not that it mattered much. He was on the way out, Molloy. It's the mid-sixties I'm talking of now. Things were looking up by then. Lamass was playing poker over Cafollas' in O'Connell Street, Westland Row was being renamed Pearse Street Station and we clapped hands till Daddy came home for the last time.

He moves forward.

The American factory with the shiny gold sign at the gate was his destination, the new blue overalls, the strange feel of him coming home every evening, the travel-light bag hanging from a nail in the shed where he took his spade after tea and joined the chorus of rural accents across the ruck of hedges in the long gardens.

He cups his hands to shout in a West of Ireland accent:

'Go on, Roscommon. Call them spuds, eh? It's the Kerr's Pinks you want.'

He straightens up.

They lived for the provincial Gaelic results and *The Waltons* radio programme.

Raises hands in declamatory pose to give the radio announcer's famous closing line:

'And, remember, if you feel like singing, do sing an Irish song.'

He moves down the centre stage.

Meanwhile Molloy marched us up and down that yard behind a 1798 pike, hustling us to try on skirts . . . for the 1916 anniversary pageant in Croke Park. RTE cancelled *The Fugitive* to show us the Easter Rising and we almost shat ourselves, Shane and Mick and me, watching the GPO burning, your man from 'Glenroe' on the television, Dinny Byrne, singing 'God Save Ireland', riddled with bullets while he plugged his last few Brits.

He has fallen to his knees, impersonating a rebel firing a revolver. Now he joins his hands and kneels in prayer.

We knelt down at night, like Pearse at his trial said he had as a child, and pledged our lives' blood for Ireland. It was all we lived for, to grow up and die for Ireland. But in the meantime we played soccer in the back field where Molloy couldn't find us and rant at how ungrateful we were . . .

He raises and wags his finger, impersonating Molloy:

'. . . the chosen generation free at last to live in your own land and yet turning your backs on your heritage, living only for that foreign game.'

He walks towards his bags and speaks in his own voice:

No different than that played by the children of those who had been forced to leave before Westland Row became Pearse Street Station.

He pauses and puts his bags on his shoulder as though about to go, then thinks.

Where was the first foreign station? Liverpool Street in '81, the time we lost in Wembley. First time the three of us had been abroad. Wound up down in the Windmill Theatre, of course. Down below five hundred Japs, up on the balcony two hundred Irish supporters on our best behaviour.

Cups hand to his mouth and shouts:

88

'Get them off you, ya brasser! Jaysus, it's wider than the Mersey tunnel.'

His own voice:

This sleazebag in a suit kept announcing . . .

He stands to attention and speaks with sleazy accent:

'Gentlemen, if all noise does not cease, the girls will not resume.'

His own voice:

We all shut up then for a while, till this girl came on as the Roman centurion and started off with the whip. Shane stood up.

Shane's voice with mock innocence:

'Jaysus, you wouldn't see the like of that in the Riordan's!'

He drops the bags beside the left-hand pole and speaks in his own voice:

They wouldn't give us a refund, but at least we got out easier than we got out of Wembley. The hatred there, the naked aggression.

He sits down on the seat.

After that it was Holland, the '82 World Cup campaign. The 2-all draw. Central station, Amsterdam. Hippies with cobwebs growing out of them busking on that square outside the station where the trains stopped. The Flying Dutchman and the Bulldog to our right, the red light and Chinatown to our left. We went right for drugs and left to smoke them.

He takes a long imaginary puff on a joint.

They were the flatland years, Shane finishing off his time with the ESB, Mick up in the industrial estate, me thinking I was set up for life in that Japanese plant. Seemed to spend every night in Dublin being kicked out at closing time. (*Grins, remembering.*) The time after we drew in Rotterdam the pub was so jammed with Irish supporters that we spilled out on to the pavement with our glasses. Next thing we know at two in the morning the squad cars arrive.

Shane's accent:

'Feels just like home, lads . . .'

His own voice:

. . . Shane said. They got out and – I'm, not joking – pushed us *back into* the pub. (*Spreads hands.*) I mean, how much culture shock can you take?

Shane's accent:

'I could get to like this country . . .'

His own voice:

Shane said. (*Sudden sourness.*) I wonder if he has?

He rises from the seat.

After that what? Belgium, Malta in '83, Windsor Park – least said the better. It became the only holidays we took. No more scuttery stations in the bog. Now it was here, following the lads, coming home like heroes to tell our mates about it. (*Pause.*) That time we played the Danes Mick suffered his first intimation of mortality. We hit Amsterdam first and found the only snooker hall in the gaff. He fluked a long red.

He bends to pot an imaginary ball and speaks in Mick's accent:

'It must be me birthday . . .'

His own voice as he straightens up, surprised:

. . . he said in a rare moment of speech. Begob, it was too, he was twenty-six that day. He didn't mind losing his hair. It was losing the Transalpino travel rates that killed him. Myself and Shane hit out for Copenhagen with a spare match ticket, leaving him to console himself.

He mimes rolling a joint.

That was when I noticed the change first. Three Kerry lads were trying to get a ticket outside the ground, looking like they'd just tied up a hayrick. We gave them Mick's free and heard about the time they had hitched to Malta from Tralee, when they were on the dole, to see Stapleton get the winner. Their accents were so broad we could barely follow them. 'How'd you get here this time?' I asked.

A broad Kerry accent:

'Ah, the oul bus, boy.'

His own voice, surprised:

The bus from Tralee?

Kerry accent:

'The oul bus from Munich, boy. Sure, half the factory's here.'

His own voice:

And so they were like an invisible explosion. Buses from

Munich and Stuttgart, three coaches from London, lads from
Berlin and Eindhoven, Cologne and The Hague, all milling
together with lads from Dublin, a green army taking over the
steps of the town hall across from the Tivoli Gardens. I don't
know why, but that night – after the Danes routed us –
listening to all those people in the pubs scared the shit out of
me, like an omen, like, I don't know, like the ground suddenly
starting to slide from under you.

He leans against the doorway to the exit.

Like that time in the seventies, the time they brought Stagg,
the first hunger striker, home from an English prison. Ar-
moured cars, lines of soldiers and tanks crossing the country
with his coffin to be buried under concrete like nuclear waste
with an armed guard on the grave. Sitting in the classroom
that day the three of us listened, remembering Molloy's 1798
Pike, his speeches the day Stormont fell, Dinny Byrne dying
gloriously in black and white on the box just a couple of years
before. The whole class could feel it, all of us walking home
from school in silence. Nobody needed to say it. Some bastard
somewhere along the line had been lying through their teeth to
us. Someone, somewhere . . .

He sits down on the right-hand-side seats.

We were the chosen ones, the generation which would make
sense of the last seven hundred years. Irishmen and Irish-
women, in the name of God and the dead generations, living in
our own land, in our own jobs, our own homes that our fathers
had slaved for us to inherit. Can you understand me? Back
then in the seventies. We were not brought up . . . to go. We
had a choice, we . . . ah!

He rises agitated and looks around him.

I knew everything was going to be different here. I could even learn to cope with having to register my address with the police. But it was this place which still freaked me. I remember, in my first week, asking some official if I could get a train from here to Rome.

A German accent, holding up one finger:

'*Nein*. Not for one hour.'

He drops hand and continues in his own voice:

Lourdes Stadium, the Market's Field. I used to come here just to read the timetables pasted on the wall – Paris, Berlin, Prague, Bonn, Madrid. Every city stretching out across this continent could be reached by just crossing these platforms. I remembered those names made of painted stones in the flower-beds beside the platforms and felt so cold suddenly, like I'd stepped outside something.

He looks out towards the left wing of the stage.

It was over there, three platforms down, that I met Shane last Saturday morning. A week ago, well, eight days now. Mick had flown in from Dublin the night before, non-committal as ever. He handed me a bottle of Jameson duty-free and his holiday visa for America. 'Are you going to stay over there illegally?' I asked.

He shrugs his shoulders and speaks in Mick's accent:

'Does the bear shite in the woods?'

He jumps up on the left-hand-side seats and speaks in Shane's accent:

'And it's hello to tonight's contestants – the Germanic bollox and the Quiet Man.'

His own voice:

Says Shane, getting off the train from Holland.

Shane's accent:

'Fingers on the buzzers, no conferring, please. Here's your starter for ten. Are we about to:
   (a) Collect and press wild flowers?
   (b) Add to our collection of rare barbed wire? Or
   (c) Beat the Brits, the Godless Russians and those Dutch bastards I've to work with and, in the process, suffer brain death due to the excessive consumption of noxious substances and solvents?'

His own voice:

Stop the lights.

Shane's accent:

'Shag off. You got it in one and you've won yourself a free trip to the Reeperbahn. Lead the way.'

He jumps down and steps back to lean against the advertisements behind him.

But we didn't go at first, just spent most of the afternoon hanging around here, staring down at the crowds milling round the trains. The crew-cut Yanks with haversacks the size of a small estate in Tallaght, the Canadians always in red waterproof anoraks with a maple leaf the size of Fionn Mac Coole's dick on the back, the little French girls that would put a horn up your back to scratch your neck.

He walks towards the left-hand pole again and sits down.

94

We took a *U-bahn* to St Pauli, slagging, driving each other crazy with twenty questions. Mick had one that nearly killed us – the last three sets of brothers to play for Ireland at any level from Youths up. (*Gestures as if to someone beside him.*) 'Give us a break,' I said. 'I'm not a professor of history.'

Mick's accent:

'No, they're all in the Irish squad – or should be.'

His own voice:

That gave us the first one, it was easy enough. (*He clicks his fingers.*) 'O'Learys – Dave and Pearse. Then . . . hang on, the Bradys, Liamo and what was his name? His brother, Ray, played Under-21. But who the fuck else?' We were still struggling when the train reached St Pauli.

He rises and leans forward, with one foot on the seat.

'Hughton,' I said. 'Chris Hughton had a brother played Under-21. Broke his leg afterwards – or was it somebody else's? For fuck's sake, Chris Hughton, of all the Irishmen . . .'

He puts his foot down, the good humour gone from his voice.

Though no one said it, we all knew why I skipped him over. Black and Cockney. I had fallen into the trap of the knockers. His mother was from Limerick. He could have been a first cousin to any one of us. (*Pause.*) It had seemed so odd, back in the seventies. After Tuhey, when John Giles took over for Poland. Peter Thomas was the first, I think, but he'd been in Waterford since before the Normans. Steve Heighway followed, but it was Terry Mancini that brought it home, the time Givens scored three against Russia. The bizarreness of it, this bald Cockney turning round during Amhran na bhFiann . . .

He stands to attention, turning his head sideways to whisper in a Cockney accent:

'This Russian anthem doesn't half go on.'

His own voice:

It didn't seem right somehow, like a party being spoilt by gatecrashers. Our own little club, our local heroes from the same streets as us. More and more followed, McDonagh and Micky Walsh, new faces and accents to be suspicious of.

He moves forward towards the Ausgang *sign again.*

That was when I still believed it back then. They didn't fit into my vision of Ireland. It was round the time my father came home with something extra in his wage packet. Uncle Sam was going home, the tax breaks and IDA grants wrung dry. The workers had a sit-in outside the plant. I caught a glimpse of Da on the nine o'clock news, awkward in his Sunday clothes, in a ruck of men behind the union official. There was something chilling in that for me, Da suddenly becoming a moment of history, on the screen like Dinny Byrne riddled to bits. Maybe I'd always seen him too close up, but his face on the television was like a map without names. All the to-ing and fro-ing from Westland Row, the years growing ashen from chemical dust.

He moves back towards the centre of the stage, using his hands to describe the imaginary station.

When he looked past the official towards the camera it was like he had finally reached his destination to find the station closed down, tumbleweeds blowing down the platforms, the signal box rusted and the tracks torn up.

He stops, turning his back on the audience.

Two months later, after the cortège had returned from his grave, Shane and Mick and me sat up all night, among the vast plates of sandwiches, drinking Guinness by the neck. I didn't weep; it was like cold water had entered my bloodstream. I doubted if I would ever be able to feel again.

He turns and leans against the advertisements.

Mick had the green *Oige* card we had always known. Mine was from the German Youth Hostel Federation, Shane's for the Dutch. We thought we were clever, but when we reached Stuttgart half the Irish nation had thought of the same trick. Oul lads eligible for the free travel and women who'd only see forty again on the front of a Finglas bus.

He moves forward, miming playing football as he speaks.

You know about the England match, Aldridge flicking it on to Houghton's head, Packy's saves, the nerves in shreds. After the game, when the team had finally gone in, we filed, singing, from the stadium to face the rows of riot shields and uniforms. Shane turned to us.

Shane's accent:

'Time to vacate this town, boys.'

He jumps up on to the left-hand seats and swings out of the pole.

We went to a little Spanish bar above Stuttgart. Down below us the death pangs of the British Empire, nourished by white bread and the *News of the World*, could run riot on the Königstrasse. All we wanted to do was to sit there entranced and savour it, a coming of age.

Shane's accent:

'I wonder what's Dublin like? All car horns hooting and pubs packed, I suppose.'

His own voice:

Shane said. Toners, the International Bar, the Hut in Phibsborough, I could imagine them all and yet . . . You know, like when you dream of something which is so real that when you wake you still want it to be there even as it's retreating from you. Shane went suddenly silent. We would never really know now what they were like that night because, even if we went back and they hadn't changed, we would have. And I knew, and I think he knew, that now when we said *us* we weren't thinking of those bars any more but the scattered army who were singing in every bar and hotel in Stuttgart that night.

He steps down and sits on the seat.

We drank now in stunned silence. I knew we were remembering much the same things. Winter evenings in Dalymount, Ray Tracy hanging out of Tomaszewski's jersey, Landsdowne Road in the years after, Brady's goal against France, that little jinking run, Stapleton's two against Spain in '82. And all the bedsits and flats with faltering televisions where we gathered to scream at the set for away games, the killer blow of that Belgium goal, minutes from time; when Eoin Hand was about to achieve the impossible dream of getting us to the World Cup finals. (*Pause.*) But it wasn't really football we were thinking about, it was something else, something we'd lost, that we'd hardly been aware of. That seemingly impossible dream we'd had of finally qualifying for something and coming home like veterans with stories to tell. There's no greater feeling than the feel of going home.

Shane's accent:

'Fuck it . . .'

His own voice:

Shane said, quietly to himself.

Shane's accent:

'. . . Fuck it.'

He rises, continuing in his own voice:

There would be no one to tell in Eindhoven for Shane, no one in Hamburg for me. Oh, people, all right, you could tell about the game, but the feel of it, the . . . No language could cross that gulf.

He steps back to look behind him.

Two Brits came in – harmless, anaemic-looking fuckers, burdened down with tattoos, terrified to be alone. They looked nervously at the tricolours, wondering if they'd be served. Shane beckoned them.

Shane's accent, with hands beckoning towards imaginary chairs at a table:

'Two beers for our neighbours. The poor wee pets. Sit down here, good surs.'

His own voice:

'Sur' is the Irish for lice, 'pet' the Spanish for fart. They looked at us condescendingly, while being insulted in three languages. We brought them drinks and waited, knowing they couldn't hold out long. It was the third beer before they got started.

English accents:

'Robson's a poky manager. I mean, England beaten by our own second team.' 'Yeah, I believe Ray Houghton went through Dublin on a bus once.' 'Hey, what do you call five Englishmen, three blacks, a Scot, an ape and a frog?' 'The Irish soccer team.'

He claps his hands and spreads them like an old-fashioned music-hall comic, then takes the leer off his face and raises his eyebrows.

We let them rabbit on, more cocky and self-righteous with each drink. One of them carried a huge radio.

Shane's accent, drawn out like an imbecile's:

'What sort of songs do you get on that? I've one at home, but it's so old I can only get old songs on it.'

His own voice:

Shane said. They explained patiently to him, as if talking to a retarded child, how the radio's age didn't matter, how the Irish station probably only played old songs from the sixties. The owner behind the bar was cracking up as Mick joined in.

Mick's dumb, mock country accent:

'Begob, them's great tattoos. You know, I've the old dick tattooed myself.'

English accent:

'You what, mate? You can't take your dick tattooed.'

Mick's country accent:

'Oh, I have. I've Kerry done down the side of it. You know,

like, I had to induce a wee bit of length into it for the job to be done and you only see the K and Y normally, but, sure, like on state occasions, you'll always see where I come from.'

His own voice:

The Brits were dumbstruck.

Mick's country accent:

'Ah, 'tis common enough in Ireland. I was in a hotel there last week and a bloke in the jakes had an N and Y on his.'

English accent:

'Where was he from? Newry?'

Mick's country accent:

'No, Newtownmountkennedy!'

His own voice:

They left shortly afterwards for some reason, shuffling moodily out into the night, clinging on to Gibraltar by their fingertips.

Shane's accent:

'I don't mind those wasters . . .'

His own voice:

Shane said, after a while.

Shane's accent:

'It's the ones nearer home that piss me off.'

His own voice as he ponders the word:

Home? (*Pause.*) After straggling up to Hanover for the Russian draw, we moved on towards Gelsenkirchen for the Dutch. There was no hostel in Gelsenkirchen. The nearest one I could find was out in the countryside. There was only one other Irish supporter in the gaff, so they bunked him in with us. He was seventeen, just finished the leaving cert.

Young Dublin voice:

'Staying over here. After the games are over. Head down to Munich to try and find some work.'

His own voice:

He said. (*Pause.*) The place was full of Germans, noxious, cheerful, shrill, healthy young bastards, rising at six o'clock to play volleyball outside our window. Mick sat on the step, nursing his hangover, staring at them.

Mick's accent:

'Have them little bastards no traffic to play in?'

He moves towards the Ausgang *sign and speaks in his own voice:*

Being back among Germans sobered me up. Yesterday afternoon I finally went down to the basement to the public phone. Hordes of young Germans crowded around the Coke machine, screaming. I phoned Hamburg, the click on the line, her steady German voice bringing the present back to me.

He cups his right hand close to his ear, as though holding a phone, but lets the image dissolve as he speaks.

'Frieda, are you sure? Yes, I know you've a regular, efficient

little German body . . . I'm only joking . . . I don't know . . .
What can I say? . . . Of course I'm delighted, thrilled . . . just
surprised. You thought it might take months after coming off
the pill . . . Yes, I might be back in Hamburg tomorrow night,
either alone if we lose or with the lads for the semi-final if we
draw . . . The lads . . . you'll like them . . . It's great news . . .
Ich liebe dich, too.'

He moves, stunned, back towards the nearest seat and sits down.

I went back up through the welter of German voices. I said
nothing to the lads, couldn't tell them. I knew it will be a boy,
his high Irish cheekbones, raven-black hair standing out among
the squads of German children like those in front of us. Will
he believe me when I try to tell him of Molloy, of the three of
us scrambling for the ball in that dirty concrete school yard?
As I stood in that hostel yesterday, in the arse of nowhere, I
seemed balanced on the edge of two worlds. Neither the
Dublin I had come from nor the Hamburg I would return to
felt real any more. Even Frieda's news didn't register. There
was just a gnawing in my stomach that I knew wouldn't stop
until the final whistle blew in Gelsenkirchen.

*He rises and walks towards the bag, opening it and removing the
scarf which he carefully places around his neck.*

We dressed in silence as usual this morning, wearing the exact
same clothes worn in Stuttgart and Hanover – superstitious
now, intense. We looked at each other. Where would we sleep
tonight? Munich, if we won by more than the Russians beat
the Brits, Hamburg together if we drew and the Russians won
or we lost and the Russians lost by more. And if we lost and
the Russians won? (*Pause.*) Nobody wanted to even talk about
that.

Mick's accent:

'Never felt this sick before a game,' Mick said.

His own voice:

We were nervous, but I knew it was different from any nervous-
ness we'd ever known before. This was no longer just a match,
no longer just how long the team could stay in Germany, but
how much longer we could remain together pretending our lives
were the same, that we were still part of the world of our youth.

He climbs up on to the left-hand-side seats.

We got to Gelsenkirchen, made it to the stadium down that
avenue of stones, got past the Dutch in a mass of orange on
three sides and packed into one corner of the crowd behind
Packy Bonner's goal. There were faces we knew from Hanover
and Stuttgart, faces from Dublin, faces we'd never known
before, piled in in one solid mass of green. And when it began
we screamed and we shouted and sang our hearts out for the
lads. For Packy, for Galvin running himself into the ground,
for Frankie suddenly old and making us old, holding up the
ball, snatching those few extra seconds that crawled by. Mc-
Grath rose at the far post and we rose with him . . .

He holds his scarf up with both hands.

. . . arms aloft, banners flying, dreaming, praying, watched the
ball spin from the woodwork. Jesus, how close can we get?

He lowers the scarf, writhing, and grips it in his fist.

Would this game ever end? My throat was parched, my legs
trembling, my heart frightened me. An old lad beside me tried
to sit on the concrete, no longer able to bear it. All around us
forty-five thousand Dutch roared as Gullit and van Basten
stormed forth, drowning our voices. How could we make
ourselves heard? It was like throwing stones into the sea.

He clenches his fist and looks around as though encouraging others to join him as he sings:

> 'Sing your heart out, sing your heart out,
> Sing your heart out for the lads.'

He shouts:

Ireland! Ireland! Ireland!

A lower voice:

Can the lads hear us? Do they know? Half-time came and still we lived in hope. We sat on the steps, faces white, trying to suck in deep breaths. What could be the slowest time imaginable? Forty-five more minutes in the heat of the Ruhr. The lads are knackered, you can see it in them. The Dutch passing it around, making them run for each ball. I closed my eyes and suddenly from last night a dream came back . . .

He slowly hunches down on the seat and closes his eyes, drawing himself closer in as he speaks.

. . . of walking down a corridor holding a fragile egg I had to shield from the light. It was so real I was living it again, my legs giving way as I sat down in the mass of legs on the terrace. I couldn't run or I would trip. I walked in slow motion, almost there now, only inches from the door. But dawn was breaking, cold light creeping towards me as I cupped the egg till it caught me and I could feel inside . . . the shell . . . the weight evaporating in my hand as its life went out.

He opens his eyes and looks up.

I opened my eyes as the roar went forth. Forty-five thousand voices like shrapnel, filling up my head, pounding off my skull. Oh, Jesus, Jesus, (*slowly*) Jesus! Shane's hand touched my shoulder.

He looks up as if at Shane.

'It's over,' he said. 'Over.'

He stands up.

I stood up among the silent men and women, their faces drained, and I raised my hands.

He raises his fist and screams:

'Ireland!' I screamed. 'Ireland! Ireland!' I had six minutes of my old life to go, six minutes to cheat time. The crowd joined in, every one of them, from Dublin and Cork, from London and Stockholm. And suddenly I knew this was the only country I still owned, those eleven figures in green shirts, that menagerie of accents pleading with God. Shane and Mick stand solid at my right and left shoulders. I know they are thinking too of the long trains back. The tunnel is being pulled out for the end of the match, photographers gathering down on the touchline. We lifted our voices in that wall of noise, one last time, to urge the lads on.

He raises the scarf once more in the air and screams:

Ireland! Ireland! Ireland!

He lowers the scarf, suddenly weary.

And then the final whistle blew. I lowered my head feeling suddenly old. The players sank down, knees pressed into the turf, as the Dutch celebrated. And after a few minutes when I looked around none of us were moving as the Dutch fans filed away, muted and relieved, down that avenue of stone.

He turns around to look behind him for a second.

Memoirs of PEIG SAYERS
~ from Ireland.
A
IN HIGH GERMANY

WEST

Irish
culture
great

And when they were gone we turned, solid to a man and a woman, thirteen thousand of us, cheering, applauding, chanting out the players' names, letting them know how proud we felt. I thought of my father's battered travel-light bag, of Molloy drilling us behind that 1798 pike, the wasters who came after him hammering *Peig* into us, the masked men blowing limbs off passers-by in my name. You know, all my life, it seems, somebody somewhere has always been trying to tell me what Ireland I belonged in. But I only belonged there. I raised my hands and applauded, having finally, in my last moments with Shane and Mick, found the only Ireland whose name I can sing, given to me by eleven men dressed in green. And the only Ireland I can pass on to the son who will carry my name in a foreign land.

I thought of my uncles and my aunts scattered through England and the States, of every generation culled and shipped off like beef on the hoof. And suddenly it seemed they had found a voice at last, that the Houghtons, the McCarthys, the Morrises were playing for all those generations written out of history. And I knew they were playing for my children to come too, for Shane's and Mick's, who would grow with foreign accents and Irish faces, bewildered by their fathers' lives.

All thirteen thousand of us stood on the terrace, for fifteen, twenty minutes after the last player had vanished, after Houghton had returned, forlornly waving a tricolour in salute, after Jack had come back out to stand and stare in wonder at us. Coffin ships, the decks of cattle boats, the departure lounges of airports. We were not a chosen generation, the realization of a dream, any longer. We were a hiccough, a brief stutter in the system. Thirteen thousand stood as one on that German terrace before scattering back towards Ireland and out like a river bursting its banks across a vast continent.

He steps down from the seat and puts the scarf around his neck.

I did not need to look at Shane or Mick. We knew that part of our lives was over for ever. We had always returned together once, a decade spent in a limbo of youth, poker sessions and parties in bedsits, football in Fairview Park on Sunday mornings before the pubs opened, walking out the long roads to Phibsborough and Rathmines on Saturday nights with sixpacks and dope and a sense of belonging so ingrained we were never aware of it.

He throws the pack up on his shoulder and turns, speaking in Shane's accent:

'Italy, 1990, lads,' Shane said. 'We'll be there.'

His own voice:

But we knew we wouldn't, even if Ireland was, knew we were fractured, drifting apart. Jesus, we all felt so old suddenly.

Shane's accent:

'We did it,' Shane said. 'We were part of it.'

He walks down towards the Ausgang *sign and stops, fingering the scarf for a moment and speaking in his own voice:*

I walked down to platform B17, found a carriage by myself, and when the ticket inspector came in he saw this scarf and nodded with a new respect. I remembered my father in carriages like that, perpetually coming home to his son in Ireland. But when I closed my eyes the Ireland I saw wasn't the streets I'd known or the fields he'd grown in. I saw thirteen thousand pairs of hands moving as one, united by pride. I knew Frieda would still be waiting up, with my child, my future, a tiny pearl inside her.

'Come on, train,' I said. 'Faster, faster. Take me home to her.' The lights of a dozen German towns spread out while the train sped on. And all the way here it wasn't the wheels that were chattering but the very network of tracks, carrying us all away from Gelsenkirchen, scattering us like seed across the continent, those steel lines chanting . . .

He sings as he walks towards the Ausgang *sign and exits.*

'Olé, Olé, Olé, Olé, Ireland, Ireland!
Olé, Olé, Olé, Olé, Ireland, Ireland!'

The Holy Ground

'There could hardly have been a more appropriate theatrical presentation to mark a changing Ireland ... than Dermot Bolger's double bill, *The Tramway End*, which opened to an ecstatic reception. *The Holy Ground* is a deeply affecting cameo of the Widow O Muirthile ... and Pat Leavy catches every nuance magically, affirming her personality and her warmth even in her desolation and her deprivation.'

Irish Times

'The best, saddest one-acter on offer this year, *The Holy Ground* is finely crafted in its language, admirable in intention, and in its closing moments is a work of elegiac poetry which should be seen by all.'

Sunday Tribune

The Holy Ground is a one-act play for one character, MONICA.

The action takes place in a living room in the suburb of Drumcondra, in Dublin in the late 1980s.

The Holy Ground was first staged (as part of *The Tramway End*) by the Gate Theatre, Dublin on 9 November 1990. The role of MONICA was played by Pat Leavy.

Director	David Byrne
Designer	Robert Ballagh
Lighting Designer	Nick Beadle
Design Assistant	Ian McNicholl
Technical Director	Ken Hartnett
Stage Director	Mairead McGrath
ASM	Triona Coen

The lights come up on a living room in Drumcondra, an old suburb of North Dublin. The room looks bare as if being stripped of its furnishings. There is a window with lace curtains to the left with an old armchair facing it. In the centre of the room there is a large fireplace with a red perpetual lamp and a picture of the Sacred Heart above it. The mantelpiece is littered with Mass cards in envelopes, an old-fashioned photograph of the 1950s amateur soccer team in a frame, three scrap-books, letters and newspapers and a mug of water. To the right is a small table and in front of that a hard kitchen chair facing the audience. On the floor behind the chair is another scrap-book, a box file and an accordion file and various scattered letters and pieces of paper with an almost empty black sack lying in the centre of it all. A few feet to the right is a huge ugly old television on the floor which we can see flickering. We can hear music and voices from it which we recognize as a scene from Brief Encounter. *A few feet to the right of the television is the door of the room.*

MONICA, *a woman in her late fifties dressed in mourning black, is standing by the fireplace putting papers into the half-full black plastic sack she is trailing in her hand. She stops for a moment and glances at the television, a sad smile coming on to her face as she becomes absorbed in the romantic scene being played out there. She moves slowly towards the set until she is bent in front of it, watching. Then with a sigh, she turns the sound down and leaning on the chair for support lowers herself on to her knees to pick up some of the papers there. She leans back.*

MONICA: Only two places the men in this ballroom want you,' Deirdre used to say. 'On your back and on your knees.' Myles was simpler I suppose, just wanted me on my knees. 'A simple man and great one,' was what the priest said.

She rises and moves back towards the fireplace, glancing back a moment at the television.

It's funny that. Not half the pleasure watching it now that he's gone. What was it Clarke said this afternoon, himself and his cronies here in their best suits praising him?

She impersonates the mourner's accent.

'Himself was very particular about the television. I never even knew there was a set in the house all these years.'

Her own voice.

'Please,' I said, trying to be firm. 'I want it brought in here.' (*She looks down at bags.*) That's when Clarke saw the plastic bags.

Mourner's voice, almost sharply.

'Be careful Missus. He'd important minutes there of our early meetings. Maybe we should take the papers and his letters.'

Her own voice, looking over at empty chair.

I stood up to them, Myles. You'd have never thought I'd have the courage.

Mourner's voice.

'You'll need a hand to sort them out. You'll be responsible for his memory.'

She glances fretfully over her shoulder at the armchair.

Your memory Myles? You still there? (*Pause.*) I've to keep telling myself you're gone. (*She circles the armchair, moving as if lost.*) Waiting for your footstep, looking for your shirts to wash. Hard to stop after all the years I've worn this ring.

She rubs her wedding ring unconsciously as she sits in the hard chair.

Grief, that's what they were all looking for. Me to play my part, a public tear at the church or graveside. Grief. (*Pause.*) There was a farm labourer away working in England when I was a girl. Fell to his death on the building sites. A new sergeant was in the barracks in Carlow, cycled out to his house in the rain and nearly banged the door down.

A gruff voice.

'Are you the Widow Dolan?' he shouts when the labourer's wife opens up.

Her own voice.

I am not.

A gruff voice.

'Well, you are now.'

A pause, then her own voice.

I am too. The Widow O Muirthile.

She rises and begins to walk towards the armchair.

I kept remembering the night you gave me the ring, Myles, that little flat I had in Portobello. The girls in the shop giggling about the great catch I'd got. And I had too, you were great. The Clonturk Celt. I remember cycling out to the Phoenix Park to watch you rising for the ball, that awful thud when skulls collided. And you came out of it unscratched at the final whistle and over to me. How proud I felt. Could never tell you.

She stands with her hand touching the back of the armchair as if searching for softness and reassurance from it.

I just reached up to stroke your hair and like a little boy you grinned. And that's what you were to me, a little boy in a big jersey clutching your shin-pads like trophies. So sweet after the rough mauling of hands I'd always known at the Metropole.

She turns and moves back to the fireplace to pick up the team photograph, then sits on the chair.

It was Deirdre in work who asked me to make up a foursome. Sunday, the 25th of April, 1954.

A girl's voice.

'It will either be a celebration or a wake depending on who wins,' she said.

Her own voice.

We met near Richmond Road, at the bridge over the Tolka. Swifty, her boyfriend called him. He didn't know what way to turn himself. All the way up Hollybank Road, shuffling his feet.

She looks around, impersonating Myles's voice.

'Wasn't it mighty? The match, mighty?'

Her own voice.

'What match?' I said and he almost dropped. 'Who was playing, who won?' (*She pulls a face, smiling.*) The look on your face, Myles. The indignity.

Myles's voice.

'We did. Drums, Drumcondra. We won the cup!'

Her own voice, looking down at the photograph in her hand.

This old photo shut Clarke up, made him stop fretting over your papers.

She looks up, speaking in mourner's accent.

'Bedad, soccer. Must have been your side of the family, Missus.'

Her own voice, as she points with her finger.

No. I pointed. 'That's Myles . . . there in the back row.'

Mourner's accent, incredulous, as if humouring a child.

'Myles O Muirthile. On a soccer team. Aye.'

She lowers photograph and speaks in her own voice.

'Hurley.'

Mourner's accent.

'Oh, he'd play hurley all right.'

Her own accent, firmly.

'No. Myles Hurley. That was his real name.'

Mourner's accent.

'Didn't I know the man half my life . . .?'

Her own voice.

'I was his wife.'

She rises and moves back towards the fireplace.

I thought he was a player that night. 'Deirdre, why's he called Swifty?' I asked in the ladies.

A girl's voice, giddy.

'Because he runs watching match after match like Matt Talbot racing between Masses!'

Her own voice.

We almost died laughing in the cubicle. Deirdre shuffling up and down in her dress, describing the other lads impersonating him, running with his hands in his pockets to see the kick-off of some game. 'So he's not a star. You haven't set me up with somebody rich and famous?'

A girl's voice, throwing her eyes up to heaven.

'Clonturk Celtic, Monica. Sunday mornings up in the Fifteen Acres and even then he normally plays "Left Outside" for them.'

She puts the photograph back on the mantelpiece and grows serious as she moves towards the back of his armchair.

You did me grand, Swifty. I didn't want a star. I came out and saw you sipping a lemonade, your eyes on that ugly cup the players were drinking from. You were like a child left alone when all the other kids are playing. I went over and let you talk about them – your heroes, Rosie Henderson and Kit Lawlor, until at eleven o'clock Deirdre's boyfriend had to ask you to see me home.

She looks out towards the audience.

Had he ever kissed a girl? He gave no sign of knowing how to. I didn't know what to do those first dates . . . I'd pause outside on the steps . . . waiting . . . lift up my head like . . . (*she raises her head*) so he could see I was . . . (*her voice deflates*) willing. (*Pause.*) Just to be kissed. I remember the week before I met him . . . a brute of a Galway man I had to fight off with my nails. (*She shudders as though pushing a man off.*) Still had the scratches on my legs the first time Myles asked me out. I remember (*she holds her arms up to her shoulders as though modelling a frock*) worrying about them as I was dressing before the tiny mirror, afraid of what he would think if he saw them.

She drops her hands and the smile goes from her.

No, not afraid. I was afraid of nothing then. I was . . . (*She pauses, trying to understand.*) Then why did the likes of Clarke scare me so much before? How many hundreds of people have I opened the door to and yet I could see them outside the church whispering 'Which one is Myles's wife?'

The priest made me sit in the front pew. I didn't want to. I knew what would happen, the queue stopping as somebody sympathized with the new Secretary and the person left staring into my face, wondering who on God's earth I was?

She picks up the scrap-books from the mantelpiece and flicks through them.

You would have loved it all the same Myles. TDs, Councillors, the local papers. (*Pause.*) Last night I went through them all . . .

She puts the scrap-books into the rubbish sack.

... the letters cut out under the different names you used. There was one scrap-book coded like the others, but it was empty. Page after page I turned, before it came to me. It was for your epitaphs Myles, the record of your last appearance.

She laughs sadly and places the sack in his armchair where the audience cannot see it.

The Life and Works of Myles O Muirthile, formerly Swifty Hurley of Clonturk Celtic.

She pats the bag as she speaks and then steps back, talking to the armchair.

I thought you were the silent type till the night I asked you in for tea. Then when you talked you were like nothing I'd ever heard. I remember all the names still, the teams you mentioned – my favourites were Bray Unknowns.

She moves around to the back of the chair, touching it with her fingers as if seeking a response.

I could imagine them like a lost tribe tramping down the Sugar Loaf once a year in grass skirts for the first round of the Cup. You had a smile that night, Myles, that could knock a girl down when you talked ... teeth so white. And you even forgot to be awkward.

She kneels down almost dreamily beside the armchair.

And while you talked I came and knelt beside you, leaned my head against your knee. Felt your fingers twisting little strands of my hair after a while.

Myles's voice.

'Bridesville,' you said softly, *'Bridesville.'*

Her own voice.

This is it, I thought. I'll raise my head now and he'll kiss me. This is it.

Myles's voice.

'Bridesville,' you said one final time.

She lifts her face to be kissed, speaking in her own voice.

'Bridesville,' I replied like a vow, holding my mouth up to yours.

Myles's voice.

'Lost to Dundalk once in the first round.'

She sits on the floor, deflated, speaking in her own voice.

I opened my eyes, you were staring at the ceiling.

Myles's voice.

'Shields scored a lovely goal for them.'

Her own voice.

That was it. For months. Lifting my head, waiting, wondering was anything wrong with me? Was there anybody else or did he just not know how to break it off? Felt so nice at first, like I was a piece of porcelain. But I wasn't. I was a woman of twenty-three and I wanted a man.

She rises and moves across towards the television.

'Bring me along,' I said one night, 'the next home match you're going to.' (*She laughs.*) The pleasure on your face Myles. You closed your eyes, I think you saw us forever in the moonlight, hand in hand watching Bohemians play Shelbourne. Then you opened them again and I saw your fear.

Myles's voice.

'What would "the lads" say?'

She leans forward to raise the sound on the television for a moment so we hear a snatch of dialogue, then lowers it again and straightens up.

It would have been easier to get him up the aisle than in that turnstile. I loved those lads I met the Sunday he finally brought me to see Drums away to Bohs, his friends at the Tramway End. The way they slagged him and made me welcome. Myles blushed till his neck was like the Red River Canyon, then forgot about everything and roared his head off at the Drums' defence. 'Come on,' they said after the game, 'we'll finally get this fellow inside a pub.'

She grips the top of the hard chair as though it were an arm.

He trudged along behind them as they made up to me. The jokes and songs they had, oh they were lovely lads, and in the pub I gripped Myles's hand to let him know he was the pick of them. 'Sing Myles, sing,' they said and finally he did, in the middle of the floor, clutching his lemonade.

Myles's voice, singing:

> And still I live in hopes to see
> The Holy Ground once more.

Her own voice.

124

'Fine girl you are!' his friends shouted the chorus and winked at me. 'Myles, what's the Holy Ground?' I whispered.

Myles's voice.

'Ireland,' he said, 'the holy land of Ireland.'

Her own voice.

And now a song from Monica, they demanded. I gripped his hand and, closing my eyes, sang what my mother used to sing me to sleep to.

She sings

> Oft in the stilly night
> Ere slumber's chains have bound me
> Fond memories bring the light
> Of other days around me . . .

She sits on the word 'stilly', her face suddenly drained, her voice faltering away to a whisper.

The stilly night, Myles. The stilly night. I overheard two of them at the graveside.

Mourner's harsh accent.

'Cold as a fish. Not an ounce of grief in her.'

Her own voice.

Didn't I grieve often enough for you in the stilly night below me here on your knees before the perpetual lamp of the Sacred Heart? Lying awake through the joyful and sorrowful mysteries, wondering. Then half asleep, hearing your foot on the stair. One step, two step, the bogeyman is coming. Waiting for the pause on the landing. Would you turn the handle?

She rises quickly as if banishing the thought and walks to the right of the mantelpiece to get a green cardigan which she pulls on, shivering as if suddenly cold.

Who would have thought back then? The day we walked all the way out to the Poolbeg lighthouse with you not speaking. Me thinking, this is it, we're going to break up.

She crosses to the fireplace.

My heart was down in my boots because . . . you made me feel special Myles, not just a heifer at a mart. You turned to me – I'll never forget that stare – like you were about to commit murder. Then I knew suddenly. You were helpless. You didn't know what to say. 'Myles,' I said. You closed your hand over mine.

She joins her hands and, bringing them up to her chest, rubs them against each other, looking suddenly deeply vulnerable.

And when you took it away I felt the shape of the box. I didn't know what to say . . . so I said 'Yes.' Just like that. Looked at you there, like you were about to blubber and I loved you, Myles. You were my child, under that big frame, and I swore I'd look after you and keep you from harm.

She lowers her hands.

He had everything planned. He was good that way – deposits, instalments. I didn't know the half of it. There was no need for me to. This house within a roar of Tolka Park, this same furniture . . . all calculated, down to the shilling. The table and chairs already bought. The beds from his mother's farmhouse. The cradle that had been his.

Her voice grows suddenly cold as she reaches a hand out, rocking it in her imagination.

I hated that. From the day he showed it to me, upstairs in the spare bedroom, alone in the corner . . . the bare floorboards, the window with no curtains. I don't know why it scared me so much. He'd kissed me a dozen times and now suddenly it was there, waiting to be filled. I wanted to tell him to put it away, take it out when the time came. But he stared at it, like . . . an obsession and I could say nothing.

She withdraws her hand in horror.

I dreamt of it that night. Rocking by itself, empty in an empty room. (*Long pause.*) Empty in Siobhan's room. It was the most crazy thing . . . when the priest was reading the burial rights, I looked up, half expected Siobhan to be there and little Simon, tiny figures at the back of the crowd, waving goodbye to their Daddy. Why . . . it's been years since . . .

Her voice falters, agitated, and she picks up the second black plastic sack, moving again as if lost, looking for something to put into it. She drops the sack and sits on the hard chair, twisting the ring on her finger.

Our wedding night he was so gentle. Only other person I ever slept with was Deirdre, sharing that little flat when we first came to Dublin. I missed her now and the girls in work; fingering his socks, wanting to ask someone how often to wash his pyjamas. The little names we had for each other, the way we'd make excuses to go to the bathroom. Sometimes we were so polite we'd start giggling at the table. So little I knew about men really, so little if anything he knew about women. He came in from a match and looked at my face.

Myles's terrified voice.

'Oh, my God, are you in pain, is it a miscarriage?'

She rises, speaking in her own voice as she moves towards his arm-chair.

'Myles,' I said, 'it's my friend has come.'

Myles's voice baffled.

'Deirdre?'

Her own voice as she stands in front of the chair.

'My time of the month Myles. Women bleed, it's painful, do you understand?' I could see his face clouded.

Myles's voice.

'Did I do wrong? Does that mean . . .?'

Her own voice.

'It takes time,' I said. 'Time.'

Myles's voice.

'When can we try again?'

Her own voice, moving to stretch her hands up on to the mantel-piece with her back to the audience.

Those few days Myles, you were someone else. Then, when it was time, you were rougher, I wasn't ready. It was . . . more like a challenge. It hurt. (*Pause.*) And every time it hurt more.

She turns around, recovering herself, and glances down at the old newspapers at her feet.

'Gusey Goose and Curly Wee.' They were Simon's favourites. Waiting all day for his Daddy to bring home the *Irish Independent*. Ah, but my stories were better than any cartoon. Siobhan never tired of hearing about when I was a young girl.

She tentatively moves to address the front of his armchair.

'We're still so young. A year isn't long. There's doctors. A check-up . . . for us both. Myles?'

She looks out across the chair towards the audience.

I went alone those first two times. Felt guilty just sitting in the queue. The second time there was a pregnant woman across from me. Couldn't bear to look at her . . . it shamed me.

A booming, refined accent.

'Why doesn't your husband come, Mrs Hurley?'

She laughs, speaking in her own voice.

Oh, it was years before I got the joke.

Refined accent.

'Why doesn't your husband come?'

She moves to the window, gazing out through the curtain.

The dreams of Monica.

She turns back to gaze at the chair.

You were my dream Myles, the only dream I every knew. This little house in Drumcondra, the crooked street lamps, the funny dog next door. All I had ever been taught to dream of. Deirdre and the girls fussing when I left work, demanding that I bring the first child down for them to see. They were your dreams too Myles, putting your bicycle in the shed, black boots running down to greet you, the excited squeal of voices. And you on the sideline one day roaring Simon on, him living out your dream in the black and green of Clonturk Celtic.

She crosses the stage.

Maybe I should never have badgered him to go. Might have been better . . . if we'd never known. Sitting in that chair when he came back.

She walks back nervously to stand with her fingers spread inches from the back of the armchair.

Shoulders so stiff. I stood behind him. And I was afraid to touch his arm . . . like it was coiled up, waiting to smash something. My little boy was gone, so deep in there he could never come out. I didn't want to see his face, afraid of what I'd see in those eyes.

She grips the chair, imitates his harsh voice.

'You call that a doctor? Oul Jackeen, trained in England. West British pup!'

She backs away from the chair.

That was all you said Myles, you never mentioned it again. But you rarely mentioned anything now. That silence, both of us sitting here . . . you in your chair, me by the fire, laughter of children in the lane. Oh, if you could only have screamed, Myles, I could have run to you. But you just ate your dinner in silence and were gone. Meetings, committees, training. You were like a savage on the football field then, somebody told me once. Blind courage they called it. It was blind rage I knew. You'd come home, cuts on your forehead, bruised eyes. You'd strip to the waist in the kitchen – I never saw you naked. Once . . . your face streaked with blood . . . I tried to help you.

She raises her hand as though holding a cloth to this head.

You flinched when I touched your forehead, stared at me. Oh good Jesus, Myles, I'll never forget that look.

She shudders and moves to the television, watching it for a moment with no sound, then straightens up, speaking in Deirdre's voice.

'Look at the state of you,' Deirdre said, 'dressing like an old woman and you only twenty-seven. It's that queer fellow has you this way.'

Her own stiff voice.

'That's my husband you're talking of, and I don't see anyone in a hurry to throw a ring around your nose.'

She sits down in the hard chair.

I had to say it to her. Lord I was desperate to talk to someone but I still carried his name. She went to England after, never saw her again or any of them. What could I have said to them? It was the time, it was our duty. Children on the street, children in prams. Balls bouncing off walls, skipping ropes in the lanes, trolley-car wheels sparking on the pavement. Every sound taunting the pair of us. Did I even think of leaving him? Where would I have gone back then? What welcome awaited me in Carlow? What scuttery room in Cricklewood, looking over my shoulder terrified to meet somebody I'd know? I had everything I had been taught to pray for . . . except a child and the love of a man. I prayed to win that back, with all my heart, all my soul.

She rises and moves to centre-stage.

What did they say to him down at training that night? It was just a joke I'm sure, some tiny slight.

Joking male voice.

'No young centre forwards, Swifty? You'd better get the lead out of your pencil!'

She looks towards the door as if he had entered and was walking past her.

I knew by your face when you came in. Waiting for you to give me the boots as usual to clean. You went out to the shed instead, hung them there on a nail. 'What's wrong, Swifty?' I said.

Myles's voice, furious.

'My name is Myles! And it's O Muirthile!'

Her own voice, distressed.

O Muirthile! (*Pause.*) I never saw you handle those boots again.

She starts packing the loose papers on the floor into the plastic sack. She picks up the accordion folder and, putting it on the chair, glances at the papers inside it. She straightens up to look at the audience.

You know the Yanks you see in O'Connell Street on Patrick's Day, always wanting to meet 'The Little People'. If they only knew, they wouldn't have far to go. In the door of the GPO, second hatch on the right after the statue of Cuchulainn. Myles and thousands like him, little people in little jobs, lives bounded by foolscap paper and elastic bands.

She puts the folder into the sack with the other papers.

There was no harm in him, all he ever wanted to do was hold his head up like any other man. You couldn't think of him opening his mouth to anyone. He was made for that life as much as I was. The longing we shared that we could never speak of. Sweet Lord, the ache in my belly like a phantom pain, the dreams of morning sickness like honey on my throat.

She grips the chair for support.

That night you hung your boots up I knew you were awake. I was praying in the dark, the Little Flower, my namesake, St Monica. Begging them to show me how to win back your love. I traced my finger lightly down your hip bone.

She cannot stop herself shuddering as she speaks slowly in a tone almost as if she was praising him for his restraint.

That was the only time he ever struck me.

She crosses to the window and looks out.

'The Dreams of Monica.' You'd sneer when you'd say it. A home, someone to love, a child ... (*Her voice grows more desperate*) Myles it doesn't even have to be ours. We could ...

Myles's voice as she turns.

'Are you mad, woman! Don't think I don't hear you, up in that spare room talking away to yourself!'

She fights to put herself back together.

That's what I was, a crazy woman inventing children for herself. Oh, God forgive me, but who else had I to talk to from dawn to dusk? What priest wants to hear? The coughing and shuffling of pews on a Friday night, people wanting to be home for their tea, the face like a blurred ghost in that little mesh of light in the confessional.

She crosses the stage and resumes packing papers away.

I'd liked his friends I'd met at the Tramway End. Simple, honest lads who made me laugh. But those lads were gone and forgotten now like the Leinster Senior League.

She straightens herself, letting the sack slip from her hand.

It was The Legion of Mary now and the Men's Confraternity. The first night he was like a man on a date, so flustered and worried he even spoke to me.

Myles's voice.

'Am I presentable, woman, or do I look a show?'

Her own voice.

The thrill on his face when he came home.

Myles's voice.

'I'm keeping the minutes, they know they can trust me!'

Her own voice.

It seemed to make him happy again, and I was glad for him and proud. (*Pause.*) Proud and alone. Reading women's magazines furtively when he was out, waking up scared he'd find them or the photo of Deirdre's little girl hidden among the old tins of Brasso and paint in the shed. The only letter she ever sent. What could I have written back? About all the years that followed? All the Ash Wednesdays and Good Fridays? Having my dresses inspected and make-up banned. And every Sunday walking to Mass, feeling him put his hand stiffly in mine.

Myles's voice.

'That new priest is a pup with his Vatican Two. We're moving the committee lock, stock and barrel.'

Her own voice.

'Where?' I asked.

Myles's voice.

'Here! My own living room. Mr Clarke, the chairman, asked for a volunteer and everyone looked at me. That's trust for you! They're important people. Don't speak unless you're spoken to. Just take their coats and stay out of the way.'

Her own voice, as she moves around demented.

I scrubbed the lino in the hall, I washed the step, I ran to the mirror like a woman demented. So long since anyone had been to the house, I had almost forgotten how to hold a conversation. At nine o'clock I served tea to the men and women here, who peered at me like an unclean animal.

She approaches the back of the chair, anguished.

What had you told them Myles? (*Pause.*) You'd told them nothing. Did I exist at all? When we were alone you'd talk to the evening paper.

She resumed packing as she speaks in his voice.

'"The 70s will be red!" Over my dead body. It's no wonder the country's destroyed with the like of them plays. We'll have a picket on that.' (*A snort.*) 'A doctor on the censorship board? Encourage every class of pornography so they can legalize the pill and make money on prescriptions for it!'

Her own voice, approaching the back of the chair again.

Oh, you thrived on that anger, touring bookshops, being abused by cinema queues. No lover could have given you such pleasure . . .

She grabs the chair suddenly and violently swings it around so the audience can see the plastic sack of papers sitting in it.

. . . no goals by Kit Lawlor or Rosie Henderson!

A pause as she goes to sit on her own hard chair.

Why were you so frightened of change? Any change, anywhere. Hoarding things in the shed, things you'd never use again. And I was worse, startled on the buses when the conductor asked for the fare as though I hadn't even expected him to notice me there. Who would have thought me capable of anything? (*Pause.*) But the night he taunted me about them, I murdered Siobhan and Simon in their sleep, over and over in my dreams, their little faces turning blue under the pillows. 'I will not go mad here,' I said, 'I will be sane, sane.' I was sane for twenty stale years. (*She looks towards the chair.*) If I could kill the children that I loved, Myles, even if they only existed in my head, then I should easily have been able to murder you.

She is silent for a moment, recovering herself.

A great man, the priest said. Great, but I could barely recognize him now.

She rises, approaching his chair as if challenging him with the words as she speaks in a country accent.

'Bravo to an tUsual O Muirthile for his letter about the pill. It's men like him we need to stand against the foreign tide of muck. – A Mother of Five.'

She stops, speaking in her own voice.

Nobody could even talk to you now, schisms and intrigues plotted in our living room. The scrap-books started for the letters to the papers under different names. When your writing grew too familiar you made me copy them. 'Cork Mother of Five', 'Dublin Mother of Seven'. Every time you made me sign myself that I cried.

She turns back to grip her own chair for support.

Every other humiliation I could take, I had been obedient like my parents had taught me, but in my room I cried and in the shops I heard the whispers.

She sits down, pausing.

It was an accident the first time, rats in the shed. Myles had the poison on a shelf in the kitchen. My elbow slipped. It covered his cabbage like a fine dust. I was about to throw it out when I stopped. I looked inside and saw him crouched at the table like an alarm clock about to go off. I wiped most of the poison off, poured his favourite gravy and served it to him. Just a speck left, Myles. No real harm meant, like a waiter spitting into the soup. But God, that night the thoughts I had of you, lying stiff in the spare bedroom. Autopsies and squad cars coming for me. All the next day I thought of prison. Would it be any different from the way I lived now? (*Pause.*) I could have gone out at nights, bingo or . . . but I'd have felt so strange there, so . . . exposed. I felt safe here in this house, for years it was all I'd known. Watching television in the kitchen, hunched up (*she hunches her shoulders*) like a cat with my finger near the knob and the sound turned amost off in case he'd return. I loved the company of it. Almost died the night I heard his voice there.

Myles's voice.

'Marriages are made in heaven, divorces in hell.'

Her own voice.

That time all around the elections and the divorce referendum,

137

the government unstable, always falling. TDs and Senators calling to the door, promising him anything for his seal of support. That photographer who snapped us for the *Sunday World*. I remember blinking in the light and looking back into the kitchen where Clarke and the others watched. Oh God, I felt so unclean and bewildered, wanting to hide away with the photo of Deirdre's girl in the shed.

She rises and walks to the fireplace, resuming her packing.

Then the elections finished . . . it was like the news on the telly . . . the wars they stop showing so you forget they're going on. (*Pause.*) That was you Myles, letters unprinted, phone calls not returned.

She stops packing and looks up.

I've never harmed a hair of anyone. So what made that thought return?

She moves back to her chair, thinking and then sits.

That young mother in the supermarket with the freckled little girl, the image of Deirdre's. She'd pinned a little badge on the child. When she saw me reading it and I smiled she smiled a little defiant smile back, as if to say we'll beat them, we'll live our own lives yet. That arm (*she raises her right arm*) I would have cut off just to go for coffee with her like I've seen other women do, to play with the little girl, to talk to someone. (*Pause.*) The badge on the little girl said 'Spuc Off'.

She rises, suddenly overcome with laughter that is close to tears.

'Spuc Off.' I started laughing, the cashiers looking up with startled eyes. 'Spuc Off! Spuc Off!' Oh God, I laughed, the tears down my face. A space cleared around me and the young woman touched my elbow.

A concerned female voice.

'Are you all right? Can I get anyone . . . your husband?'

Her own voice.

'My husband is dead,' I said, 'thirty years dead. Swifty Hurley, he was a good, simple man, a footballer.' I left the shop and almost ran home. I felt the whole street was looking at me. I took the poison from the shed, put it above the cooker and made his favourite stew.

She cries out softly.

Oh Swifty, my only love! You were my husband, what would I be when you were gone?

She sits down in the chair.

All the things people kill for. Money and God and countries. I killed for companionship, can you not understand? Those rough women in prison, they didn't frighten me any longer. Four of us crammed in a cell, at least they would have to talk to me.

She rises again and picks up the now full black sack on the floor, speaking in a mourner's voice.

'You'll be responsible for his papers, Mrs O Muirthile. When can we call for them?'

Her own voice as she carries the sack over to the door.

'Eleven o'clock on Tuesday, Mr Clarke,' I said. Remember Myles, the binmen are always gone by half-ten.

She exits to dump the sack outside and then re-enters.

Even Clarke and his friends spuced off on you these last months Myles, new offices down town, computers and spokesmen in smart suits.

She lifts the second sack from the armchair and begins to cross to the door again.

They left you alone to struggle with your own Calvary. Wandering the streets with nobody heeding you, having rows with young people sniggering on the bus home. How long would it take the poison to work? I threw it out the next morning but it was there inside you. I wanted to tell you, to warn you, but . . . Myles, all these years we've barely spoken. You'd come home late and I'd hear you down here singing old hymns to yourself.

She pauses at the door and looks back in.

This was when you finally needed my help, an overwrought little boy blubbering away to yourself. But you had killed every feeling inside me until I just lay there numb.

She exits to dump the sack and comes back to stand in the doorframe.

I woke on Tuesday and knew something was wrong. The little sword of light under my door almost paled with dawn. And every step I took seemed a descent into nightmare. I stood outside this door, Myles, and realized . . . I wasn't afraid you were dead, I was afraid you might still be alive. You were slumped here in front of the perpetual lamp (*she looks down at the carpet*), a grotesque, pitiable figure. All the years in the GPO, Myles, the second hatch on the right after the statue of Cuchulainn. It wasn't Rosie Henderson I saw now, but that statue of a warrior dying, tying himself to a rock. For half an hour I stood in this doorway like the men of Ireland, afraid to approach, not daring to call your name in case you'd look up. Then . . . I went walking through the streets in my slippers and dressing-gown.

She crosses stage to stand beside his armchair.

Outside the Mater Hospital two nurses appeared. They brought me inside and phoned an ambulance. 'Was it the rat poison?' I kept asking, 'the rat poison?' I wanted to be charged, to be taken away.

She pauses, trying to remember the word.

What was it the doctor called it? *'Warfarin.'* I think that was the name.

A strong male voice.

'Your husband died from a clot to the brain. The man had a history of thrombosis, he'd take treatment from nobody. Rat poison contains warfarin that prevents clotting and thins out the blood. If you did give it to him you probably lengthened his life. Go home now Mrs O Muirthile and keep your mouth shut.'

She sits down in his armchair for the first time.

Sweet Jesus, Myles, what sort of wife was I? I couldn't make you happy in life and I couldn't even send you to your death. They thought it was for you I was crying but it was for me. Because how can I cope thrust out into the world, how can I learn to watch that (*she glances towards the television*) without hunching up beside it, to walk out into the evening like an ordinary person? To learn to play bingo and sit in the park, to chance a conversation with a kind person on a bus?

She seems to sink further and further into the armchair.

The doctor sent in an old nun in white robes to comfort me. She pressed her hands in mine. 'Pray,' she said. Those kind eyes she had, she made me feel warm. 'Our Father who art in heaven,' she began. I closed my eyes and thought of God. I saw him there kindly ... like my own father beckoning but suddenly you were there beside him, Myles, righteous and stern.

The lights have gone down until there is just her lost in a dim spotlight.

I tried to pray but nothing would come. You've stolen my youth and left me barren, you've stolen my gaiety and gave me shame, and when I die I will die unmourned. But I could forgive you, Swifty, everything except that ... seated there at the right hand of God, you had stolen my Christ away from me.

The set fades into darkness.

ONE LAST WHITE HORSE

'Bolger is angry and compassionate, understanding and scath-ing, raw and lyrical as he traces Eddie's life-cycle with bleakly powerful authenticity, and mirrors a society at an advanced stage of moral decay and spiritual emptiness. An extraordinarily fine piece of theatre.'

Irish Independent

'Full of revelatory detail and pulsating anger, it is certainly better than any new play I have seen in a London fringe theatre this year.'

Observer

'One does not expect to be entranced and uplifted by a play about a homicidal crack addict whose beloved elder brother dies of AIDS, but I was. I found it worked superbly.'

Financial Times

CHARACTERS

EDDIE

FATHER

HORSE

OLD MAN

EILEEN

MAUREEN

BRENDAN

SMILER

SHERIFF

TRAMP

For Padraig J. Daly

One Last White Horse was commissioned by The Abbey Theatre and first staged by them in Dublin on their Peacock Stage on 8 October, 1991. The cast was as follows:

EDDIE	Owen Roe
HORSE	Barbara Brennan
EILEEN	Hilary Fannin
BRENDAN	Liam Cummingham
FATHER	Des Braidan
MAUREEN	Bernie Downes
SMILER/SHERIFF	Donal O'Kelly
OLD MAN	Peadar Lamb
TRAMP	Macdara Ó Fátharta

Director	David Byrne
Music	Gerard Grenell
Designer	Brownen Casson
Lighting	Tony Wakefield
Stage Manager	John Stapleton

The play is set inside the head of a young man in Dublin in the mid-1980s.

ACT ONE

Both the left and right backdrop of the stage consist of the looming shapes of railings that – in as much as they resemble anything – seem like broken bars of corporation railings around a waste ground. They have a distorted, surreal feel to them.

The main stage area itself is an uneven surface, possibly a vividly splattered cloth suggesting a waste ground with the remnants of earlier wild vegetation merging with dumped rubbish. However this is suggested more by feel than any sort of actual realistic detail. There is in the centre of the stage an old wardrobe which actors can sit on and which also serves as a sort of physical divide. There is a ramp made up of a broken door at the back left of the stage, beside an entrance like the broken doorway of an old house at the back centre, through which the actors enter. At the front there can be one or two other objects, such as a broken bicycle frame, to suggest a waste ground; but inasmuch as we are dealing with anything it is the landscape of dream, where juxtapositions can occur without comment, where the sole logic is the logic of the dreamer. Inasmuch as is possible, the clothes of the actors should likewise be recognizably real and yet sufficiently distorted to heighten the surreal, nightmarish quality of the play. This quality is further heightened by the soundtrack, which is woven in and out of the text.

The stage begins in black-out and then just enough light bleeds in for us to make out the form of EDDIE, *just visible as he stumbles on clutching a small bag. He is in his mid-twenties, smallish and thin-faced with closely cropped hair. He is wearing jeans and a thick bluish shirt. He looks around him, dazed, as if*

trying to identify where he is or to search for something or make a
decision. As he paces the stage we realize that his increasingly
aggravated movements are him trying to shake off the voices
inside his head.

EDDIE: (*Angrily, almost to himself*) I can be rid of your voices.

(*He dumps the bag on the wardrobe and opens it to take out a*
child's T-shirt which he unfolds to reveal a few pieces of
broken pottery. He replaces them in the bag and dumps his
works out on to the wardrobe: a small candle, a spoon,
matches, a hypodermic syringe, a Jif plastic lemon and a
packet of white powder. He lights the candle, undoes the belt
from his jeans and straps it round his left arm and pulls it
tight with his teeth for a moment. He slaps at his arm to find
a vein, then empties the bag of powder on to the spoon,
squeezes some lemon juice into it and heats the spoon over the
candle flame. He fills the syringe from the spoon and, lifting it
up, sits on the wardrobe. He slaps his arm again, pulls the
belt tighter with his teeth and plunges the needle into his arm.
The moment the needle touches his flesh a brilliant white light
is thrown on the figure of the HORSE *– a woman in a white*
shroud-like robe which, when she lifts her hands, spreads out
to form a cloak – who has appeared at the entrance behind
him and begins to circle EDDIE.)

HORSE'S VOICE: Will you lift the needle to the moonlight,
see the tip glisten like a snake's tongue? And pull the strap
tighter and slap hard for a vein? And wait till it stands out,
bulging and blue and screaming to be filled? And let those
steel lips open so I can enter into you?

(*As the heroin drains into* EDDIE's *arm the* HORSE *grips his*
outstretched left hand and draws him into an embrace by
cradling his head as he lets it fall back.)

I've been saving it for you all day son, I knew how
thirsty you would be. Lemonade! See how the light flows
through it like it were champagne. The longing inside
you is so much you can almost taste the bubbles bursting
on your tongue. Throw your head back, son, throw it
back.

(*She lets go his hand, moving her own hand back slightly out of his reach as though taking a glass away from him.* EDDIE *is almost gagging with the strain of trying to swallow, as he tries to connect his hand again with her own. He gasps suddenly and stares down at the empty needle in his hand which drops from his grasp. The* HORSE *lowers her hand and smiles.*)

Can you not see, son? It's a trick glass, a trick.

(*She backs away and* EDDIE *slumps down on to the wardrobe as the stage plunges into a harsher light. The* HORSE *has vanished back into the shadows.* EDDIE *now looks more glazed, unsure of where he is.* EILEEN *comes forward to stand at the side of the wardrobe.* EDDIE *slumps forward again and, reaching a hand out, touches her. He pushes himself towards her, pressing his arms around her waist as she stands motionless.*)

EILEEN: Are you happy now, Eddie?

EDDIE: Am I with you now, Eileen?

EILEEN: (*Sadly*) No Eddie, you are gone from me for ever.

(*He raises his eyes to look at her, reaching for her hands.*)

EDDIE: The buffeting has stopped, the ache tormenting every vein. Used to feel once like . . . like I was flying at this stage. Our living room gone, the quiz show on the television gone, the noise of the kids on the street drifting away.

EILEEN: And you drifting away with them from your wife and your child. Little Orla staring at you as you sat on the sofa not even waving day-day to her.

(EILEEN *backs away from him.*)

EDDIE: You left me Eileen.

EILEEN: No, Eddie. I would never have left you.

EDDIE: Remember how I was in those early months when we met. A tiger in a crumpled sweatshirt, afraid of nothing, taking lip from nobody.

EILEEN: You were my love.

EDDIE: What did you think about then when we fucked? Could never tell, your face like a secret.

EILEEN: I thought of you, Eddie.

(EDDIE *lies back on the wardrobe, then slides off it and leans against the side looking at* EILEEN.)

EDDIE: I thought of horses. (*He laughs.*) I mean at the end when I was coming. When I couldn't control it any more, my legs trembling, everything giving way. The last white horse on the last headland. The last wild one and I'm riding her bareback as she carries me on and on into the light and then I'd come, little gasp of breath, open my eyes and look at you looking up.

EILEEN: I thought of you, Eddie, the sweat on your shoulder-blades, the way that I could feel your sharp bones pressing in on me.

(EDDIE *rises and approaches her.*)

EDDIE: Never unfaithful to you since that first night under the stairway of the flats. You frightened your mother would come out. And the way you let me keep your knickers afterwards, soft in my palm in my pocket, and me thinking of you coming in, your father and brothers in armchairs watching the football as you passed through them to your room.

EILEEN: With nothing beneath my dress except the feel of you still there after you had gone, the scent of rubber so strong in my nostrils I was frightened they would smell it, and running to look out the window at you crossing the courtyard. Me in the dark with my little sister asleep in the bed. Oh, Eddie, Eddie, Eddie.

EDDIE: I want to be back with you.

(*He lays his hand gently on her breast.*)

EILEEN: Eddie, I told our child that you had died.

(EDDIE's *head sinks down again as she pushes his hand down and backs away. He turns back to lift the empty syringe and drops it, confronted by the* HORSE *who stands in front of him.*)

HORSE: I have stilled your body, but even I may not control your dreams.

(EDDIE *backs away again.*)

EDDIE: (*Scared*) I know your features, though it has been years since I put them away.

HORSE: If you did not why would you run back to this place? A piece of waste ground lit only by memories, black pools of oily water, an old bridge fenced off by boulders to keep the tinker's trailers at bay. You recognize more easily than I do that slumped figure kneeling on the drenched grass whom you have just left behind you?

(EDDIE *looks back towards the needle as though he could see himself as a figure lying there.*)

EDDIE: Weightless as an astronaut, then why do I still feel his pain?

HORSE: Why would he come back here Eddie if you did not know me? Dream it again, son. (*She puts her arms around him from the back.*) The clear waters of the Tolka, the Silver Spoon. Mothers clustered on the bank in the summer evening, the hiss of a crackling transistor, children splashing about in the pools.

(EDDIE *sits on the wardrobe and lifts his hand up, placing the palm out flat as if holding a slice of bread on it.*)

EDDIE: With bread and jam in our hands as we waded through the waters of a single infinite summer. And the whiteness of our bodies, ribs like rows of silvery needles. Are you my mother, have I finally come home?

(*She kneels behind him and touches his shoulder, pulling him towards her.*)

HORSE: Eddie, my son, I've your clothes here dry for you.

(*He turns towards her, shivering.*)

EDDIE: I'm cold from the water, Mammy, so terribly cold.

(*He lays his head on her shoulder and she pats his hair.*)

HORSE: Of course you are, son, and from all the excitement of this long day.

EDDIE: When are we going home, Mammy?

HORSE: Soon, son. Very, very soon.

(EDDIE *shivers again, suddenly looking very slight and anxious.*)

EDDIE: I've forgotten ... the path home, Mammy. Is it out

along the canal or down through the estates? (*Pause.*) I'm
so cold I'm frightened, Mammy, so cold I'm frightened.

HORSE: Look, son.

(EDDIE *turns so that he is facing the audience, leaning back
against her with her arms around his neck.*)

EDDIE: The last white horse. On the headland there by the
old king's ramparts beside the bottomless quarry where
the blind sharks dwell. Is there a herd of horses there,
Mammy, or is he the last living one?

HORSE: It's a mare, son, a mare. The last solitary one. All
the great oaks are felled and all the great stallions that
ran wild here for centuries slaughtered with them. Just
that broken mare left now, nosing her way through the
sacks on the rubbish dump, shying away among the last
few crooked trees on the waste ground here by the
river.

EDDIE: How do you know, Mammy?

HORSE: (*Coyly*) Oh, a little bird on a branch told me.

EDDIE: Has anyone ever ridden on her back?

HORSE: If they have, they have never returned to relate the
tale.

EDDIE: When I grow up I'll master her, cling on to her mane
and gallop at night through every sleeping street. Won't I,
Mammy?

HORSE: It's my lasting fear that you will, son.

(EILEEN *enters and* EDDIE *looks towards her, realizing that
he has moved back in time and is at home, then back at the*
HORSE *who has taken up a crouching position at his feet as
the child.* EDDIE *looks back at* EILEEN *and laughs. He leans
forward to address the* HORSE, *speaking in a soft voice.*)

EDDIE: I was a little boy and Mammy was a little girl like you,
and I lived in a house like this beside the huge tower block
where she lived with eagles nesting on the roof just below
the sky. And all the time she was your Mammy and I was
your Daddy and neither of us ever knew that we would
find each other.

(EILEEN *steps forward and approaches.*)

EILEEN: Orla, my love, it's long past your bedtime. (*She beckons as though to a child.*) Daddy will tell you more stories tomorrow.

(*She smiles as the* HORSE *rises and backs away up the ramp, freezing into the posture of a marble statue.*)

EDDIE: It's funny. Still find it hard to say that word. (*Pause.*) Mammy.

EILEEN: How old were you?

EDDIE: Seven years and eleven days.

EILEEN: I never heard you mention her, all the years I knew you, until we had Orla.

EDDIE: So little I remember. Never really gave the woman much thought, never . . . I . . .

(*He stops, suddenly distraught.* EILEEN *puts her hand on his shoulder.*)

EILEEN: Eddie, you always keep things bottled.

(EDDIE *is silent for a moment, as if forcing himself to think back.*)

EDDIE: One minute she was there beside me, talking all about the sale in Clery's, jigging my arm to hurry me on. A whole crush of people gathered at the lights by the Gresham Hotel. I let go her arm a minute, looking back at the unlit bulbs of the Christmas lights in the trees jangling in the gale. The gust of wind nearly took the feet from me before some old lad grabbed my shoulder. She lost her balance . . . I think she was so busy looking to see where I was. She toppled over like in a game of statues. Oh Christ, Eileen, Orla's eyes, they remind me of hers. I never forget her face . . .

(*The* HORSE *spreads her arms out and lifts them over her head so that her face is obscured by the folds of white cloth.*)

I think she blamed me for letting her hand go. Her eyes, never saw them like that before, like she wasn't my mother. She hadn't even time to scream. The poor truck driver was in bits, they had to take him off in an ambulance as well. 'The sale in Clery's,' they were the last words she ever spoke to me. 'The sale in Clery's.'

(*He walks forward towards* BRENDAN *and the* FATHER *who have come out from the shadows.* BRENDAN *holds his hands out for a moment and shakes his head in disbelief.*)

FATHER: She's gone, Eddie. Oh Jesus, kid, she's gone from us.

EDDIE: (*Sudden burst, near tears*) You're lying; it's just another of her jokes.

(EDDIE *turns towards the* FATHER *who is trying to control his own grief.* EILEEN *has retreated.*)

FATHER: Eddie, my youngest son.

EDDIE: You shut up. Both give over your messing. She's getting me a jacket in Clery's. I want it now, I want her to get it. She promised. A jacket in Clery's.

(*The* FATHER *moves towards* EDDIE, *but* EDDIE *brushes past him and is confronted suddenly by the* HORSE *who lowers her hands to reveal her face.*)

EDDIE: (*A note of bitterness*) You promised. Always teasing me, making up yarns. Remember that hottest and final day of autumn, clothes sticking to my back as I walked home to you, all the way up the steep hill from the Botanic Gardens. The glass of sparkling lemonade you had waiting for me on the window sill in the kitchen.

(*The* HORSE *holds an imaginary glass out.*)

HORSE: I've been saving it for you all day, son, I knew how thirsty you would be.

(EDDIE *accepts the glass from her. He cups it in his hands and throws his head right back, raising his hands to his lips and almost gagging with the strain of trying to swallow.*)

EDDIE: Sweet Christ, Mammy, the light is flowing through it like it were champagne. This longing is so much I can almost taste the bubbles bursting on my tongue. Why am I still aching for lemonade?

(*The* HORSE *reaches her own hands out to lower his and smiles.*)

HORSE: Can you not see it's a trick glass, son? Young Sheila Murphy brought it in from next door. Look at the sheet of glass inside the glass itself, isn't it clever?

(EDDIE *grimaces and makes a noise as if about to burst into tears.*)

HORSE: (*Surprised by his outburst but trying to soothe him*) You know we can't afford lemonade, son. I'll get you some nice cool water from the tap.

(*She backs away from him.*)

EDDIE: Why did it upset me so much, crying in that small kitchen, feeling so lost and betrayed? Even when you found the money to send Brendan for lemonade why did it not taste the same? I guzzled the whole bottle down, never lifting the glass rim from my teeth. But why was it like an ache inside me that could never be filled . . . like a trust broken . . . like I could never be certain of anything again? Why?

(*The* HORSE *turns her back slowly, refusing to answer as* EDDIE *sinks to his knees. He stares ahead as* BRENDAN *approaches.*)

BRENDAN: Jesus kid, it's Christmas night and the fire's dying. Standing out here in the frozen yard these last twenty minutes. I won't send you for coal again. (*He bends as if to use a shovel.*) Even the coal is stuck together, stiff with frost. Not a night for a beggar.

EDDIE: (*After long pause*) Do you remember Mammy, Brendan?

(BRENDAN *looks at him, surprised.*)

BRENDAN: (*Gentler voice*) Of course I remember her.

EDDIE: She took us to see a film once. We walked all the way to the Classic in Whitehall.

BRENDAN: Lana Turner in *Madame X*, wasn't it? Sure every woman in the street was there, every husband at home starving, wondering where his dinner was.

EDDIE: Up in the plush darkness of the balcony. Chocolate melting in my palm as the usher's torch flickered over the rows of grey faces. Do you remember where the woman had to leave her family and go tramping through the winter streets. The bit that Mammy cried at the most was on Christmas night, the woman coming back, standing in the garden to gaze in the window at them. No one looks out and sees her keeping a vigil in the snow. I don't know why, but I remembered it suddenly just now after all these years and something made me look up at the old bushes there.

(BRENDAN *glances over his shoulder, suddenly apprehensive.*)

BRENDAN: What did you see, kid?

EDDIE: Nothing. Why the hell should I? Bloody drink, I'm not used to it, like you. Just thought she might be ... Christ, I don't even know if I wanted to see anything there or not.

(BRENDAN *puts an arm on his shoulder, consolingly.*)

BRENDAN: It's been nine years, kiddo. Come on, it's time to forget ...

EDDIE: (*Abruptly*) Forget what? A bagful of old stories and scraps of prayers, a few fuzzy photographs of me miserable on Dollymount strand? I don't even remember that woman.

(*The* HORSE *has come forward to stand beside the kneeling* EDDIE *as* BRENDAN *backs away. She joins her hands in prayer.* EDDIE *looks up uncertainly and plucks at her sleeve. She motions him away with her hand. There is a pause before* EDDIE *plucks at her sleeve again. She raises a finger to her lips. There is a final pause before he looks up to whisper.*)

The Mass is over, Ma. Why are we still here?

HORSE: Your grandfather and two grandmothers, your Uncle Pete, your Auntie Joan. The soul of that poor young mother who threw herself from the eighth storey of those new flats last week. Prayer is never wasted, son. Nobody can ever know how many prayers their souls will need to escape from purgatory.

EDDIE: And so it could be my last Hail Mary of the night that would bring someone that final inch of the way. Would they know it was me who finally released them into God's light?

HORSE: They would, son, and all the forgotten souls in torment who have no one left to pray for them.

EDDIE: Mammy? (*She looks at him.*) If you died ... just

saying if you did . . . I'd say prayers on my knees for four hours every morning and four hours every night and become a robed priest when I'd grow up so I could say every Mass for you alone and you'd get into heaven in a flash without needing anybody else's help.

HORSE: But why should I die, son?

(*She smiles and begins to back away from him.*)

EDDIE: (*Confused suddenly and frightened*) No, I don't mean you should, I just mean if . . . I mean . . . I mean . . .

(*The* HORSE *vanishes into the shadows where again she stands like a religious statue, as* BRENDAN *and the* FATHER *come to stand with hands joined as if in prayer on either side of him.*)

. . . the Mass is over.

(*He rises angrily as* BRENDAN *and the* FATHER *look at him.*) I'm not going, you can't make me. I'm not a child any longer.

(EDDIE *suddenly makes a choking sound and tries to spit out an imaginary Host which has become stuck to the roof of his mouth.*)

The feel of the Host every Sunday, stuck up there on the roof of my tongue like a bit of rotten flesh that won't peel off. I'm thirteen and I won't be lied to. (*He wipes his mouth.*) I don't want it, I don't believe in it. Mammy's dead and that's the end of it.

FATHER: (*Violent whisper*) And what would your mother say to that? How does she feel watching you from heaven?

EDDIE: Not going to the grave today, there's no point, there's just skin and bones and nothing else left.

(*He turns in anger and storms a few steps away, then stops, staring ahead.*)

BRENDAN: Leave him, Da. The kid has a hole in his heart. A hole in his heart that he'll never fill.

(BRENDAN *exits leaving the* FATHER *staring at* EDDIE.)

EDDIE: (*To himself*) Nothing else left.

(*The* HORSE *sinks down, dissolving into the image of the figure at the foot of the cross.*)

FATHER: You love your sons equally, even if they're as different as your left and right arm. I never worried about Brendan, picking up work here and there. Off on that big truck he drove for the pigeon club, loaded down with caged birds, bringing me for a few pints every time he got home. You could see how Eddie wanted to be him, strutting round like a skinhead at nineteen, but he just wasn't made tough. I don't know, I was too preoccupied with my own grief to notice it creep in, but he never lost that worried look, ever since her death, like he was guilty of something but couldn't remember what.

(BRENDAN *crosses* EDDIE's *line of vision and* EDDIE *begins to follow him at a distance around the stage.* BRENDAN *stops and looks back.*)

BRENDAN: Go on with yourself, Eddie.

EDDIE: I'm going with you.

BRENDAN: Not this time, Eddie, it's a different sort of business.

EDDIE: I'm going with you.

BRENDAN: Come on, kiddo, I've seen you with that girl from the flats. There are more ways than one to work up a sweat.

EDDIE: Tell me where you're going then.

BRENDAN: It's my own business, right. (*He changes mood.*) Here, I'll arm-wrestle you, come on.

(BRENDAN *kneels at the wardrobe and puts his hand down.*)

EDDIE: You always win.

BRENDAN: Come on, I'll give you a head start. If you beat me you can come.

(EILEEN *goes to sit behind them.* BRENDAN *lowers his hand back as* EDDIE *takes it, but is still easily beating* EDDIE *when* EDDIE *lifts his eyes from* BRENDAN's *arm to gaze at his face. Their hands are locked together limply.*)

BRENDAN: A vaccination mark, kiddo, that's all. (EDDIE *doesn't reply.*) Come on, you can beat me if you try.

(EDDIE *tries to take his hand away but* BRENDAN *grips it tighter, forcing his hand forward so that* EDDIE *wins the contest.*)

BRENDAN: You won, Eddie.

EDDIE: No, I remember now . . . it happened before. I didn't win. You beat me like you always do.

BRENDAN: Don't let go my hand Eddie, don't let go my hand.

(EDDIE *prises his hand away and lifts it back over his shoulder where* EILEEN *grasps it.* EDDIE *shivers as though wakening as* BRENDAN *backs away.*)

EILEEN: Eddie, wake up. What's wrong?

EDDIE: What time is it?

EILEEN: After four, I think. I hear the kids let out from school. It will be dark soon.

EDDIE: I was dreaming, if I could only remember. It's a strange feeling . . . lovely . . . waking up beside you.

EILEEN: You're the first man I've known, Eddie, I mean that I've let go all the way. I know men feel different about it . . . conquests.

EDDIE: I went down with Brendan once to collect crates of pigeons at the Broadstone. A bloke there was bragging that he'd screwed every girl in Phibsborough except his mother and his sister. Brendan just picked up the crates and winked at him. 'Between the pair of us so,' he said, 'we've screwed them all.'

(EILEEN *laughs and they sink back on to the wardrobe. As they curl towards each other* MAUREEN *enters and stops at the doorway as* EDDIE *and* EILEEN *look up, startled and anxious, at her.*)

EILEEN: Oh Christ, it's Maureen.

EDDIE: (*Angrily*) You told me she was in The Joy doing time?

MAUREEN: I got out early, lover boy, didn't I? Two blouses fecked from Dunne's Stores. It wasn't exactly the Great Train Robbery.

EILEEN: You get dressed Eddie, I'll talk to her.

(*She sits down between them as* EDDIE *hunches up, concealing his nakedness, and pokes at his back with her foot.*)

MAUREEN: You're starting off small, sister, or is the weather just cold, lover boy? (EDDIE *covers himself, self-consciously.*) I remember you. You're the kid brother of that fellow who drives the pigeon truck, aren't you?

EDDIE: (*Staring at her eyes*) I'm surprised you even remember your own name.

MAUREEN: I had to have a little welcome-home party, hadn't I? Seeing as I wasn't invited to the one my kid sister was throwing in my own flat. Of course in my day we hadn't flats to have little parties in. No, some crooked back lane off D'Olier Street, stinking of piss and damp, young girls shivering in their party clothes floating like kites past the entrance. Being naked was a luxury in my day, the feel of wet stone against your arse and his slippery little bank-clerk's hands flailing at me in the middle of it. Is he mad or what I thought, the face of him in agony. (*Man's voice*) 'Me dick is stuck in your zip and you're going to get pregnant!' Jesus, I laughed so much I think I made him come. (*Pause.*) I laughed so hard he had to marry me.

EDDIE: Are you finished now?

MAUREEN: You see I had no big sister to look out for me, I had no one.

EDDIE: Just two kids if you could have bothered being a mother to them, eh?

(*There is a pause while* MAUREEN *stares at him. When she speaks her voice is colder, almost without expression.*)

MAUREEN: I was more a mother than you will ever be a father to my sister's child.

(EDDIE *turns as if struck as* MAUREEN *exchanges a look with* EILEEN *and exits.* EDDIE *rises and approaches the* FATHER *and* BRENDAN *who circle him as* EILEEN *retreats. The* FATHER *sits on the wardrobe. The* FATHER *looks at* BRENDAN, *who shrugs his shoulders, and then back at* EDDIE.)

FATHER: (*Half-laugh*) You want to get married? But you're still so young, son?

EDDIE: I have a job in O'Rourke's hardware shop, it's not much but it's steady.

BRENDAN: Come on, kiddo. O'Rourke's. I don't want to be cruel but . . . that cute old fox, Mrs O'Rourke. Oh, you'd swear you were her son the way she speaks about you, and you'd certainly swear she was leaving you the shop the way you slave for her, but cop yourself on.

EDDIE: She says she'll give me a letter for the bank. I've been looking at this small estate of town houses out beyond Clondalkin. I figure maybe I could get together a deposit for one.

FATHER: (*Rises*) What's your hurry, son? Is it . . . ?

EDDIE: Eileen. I don't have a choice, Da. I know what I want. To do it my own way, on my own two feet.

(*The two of them begin to back away from* EDDIE, BRENDAN's *voice losing its everyday tone.*)

BRENDAN: On your two feet was right, kiddo, eh? Two buses in from the backwoods of Clondalkin, and then, when the old biddy got sick, did you ever see home before half ten at night after visiting her in the hospital? I can just see her, kiddo, propped up by starched pillows, holding the receipts you put into her hands like they were rosary beads.

(*The* SMILER O'ROURKE *has come forward from the side of the stage as Brendan retreats. The* SMILER *walks towards* EDDIE *with a broad smile as he looks around him.*)

SMILER: Family Guard fire alarms and battery clocks, automatic clothes lines and five-lever mortise deadlocks, Wavin waste pipes, gutters and fittings, washable wallpaper only one pound, ninety-nine pence, and up on the counter by the wooden cash register *The Sacred Heart Messenger* and *An Phoblacht*.

(*He stops and gives a short laugh, looking at* EDDIE *for the first time.*)

Smile for the customers, she always said. Lord, I was never done smiling. (*Pause.*) So you're the famous Eddie, eh? The mother's never done talking about you. I remember your brother Brendan well. Still driving the pigeons, is he?

EDDIE: That's right.

SMILER: A wild man. Still it will do him no good in the end. You're the wiser man now, learn the price of everything, the value of a pound.

EDDIE: All the cash records are inside. I've had to lodge the money myself in the night safe, but you can check that every penny is accounted for.

SMILER: Sure there's no need. If the mother trusts you, then you're all right by me. (*Confidential tone*) She's in a bad way, Eddie. Counting the beads she is inside, thinking Padre Pio is going to save her. But God help her, Eddie, she's not going to leave that hospital except in a wooden box. (*He looks around and smiles.*) It was a grand shop this; you know she raised the whole lot of us from that little space behind the counter when the father died. If we weren't on our knees for the Angelus we were down rooting for nails and 6-amp fuses. And there's none of us ever wanted for anything. But of course, times change you know. It's been more of a pastime for her now these last years. Don't know why she never sold it. You can buy most of this junk cheaper down the road in the super-market. (*Pause.*) It's stone dead, Eddie, you know that?

EDDIE: I thought she managed all right?

SMILER: Ah now, what would feed an old woman wouldn't support family men the likes of you and I, eh? Sure it's the best thing to happen to you Eddie, get you out of this rut.

EDDIE: But she never said anything to me, even last night. Will I not go in and see her?

SMILER: (*Sharply*) No! (*More quietly*) It's best to leave my mother alone with her prayers now, Eddie. It's between her and Padre Pio now. She said you were a good lad, Eddie, to give you three weeks' holiday money when I paid you off. She didn't have to do that, you know, but she was always good that way.

EDDIE: But . . . I've worked . . .

SMILER: The company's gone into receivership, Eddie, but we'll not see you stuck. You stay on for the closing-down sale, everything to clear, and I'll look after you with a bit of overtime. Get you a start, you know. And I'll tell you what (*laughs*), myself and yourself now we'll write you a reference between us that will take the sight out of your eye. I'll sign it in her name for you, sure I could do a signature of hers that would pass on her last will and testament.

(*He stops and looks around him as though he has just realized what he has said, then looks back at* EDDIE *and smiles as he moves towards the doorway.*)

She should have sold it years ago. It's an obvious goldmine as a location for a video shop.

(EDDIE *stands looking after the* SMILER *who has vanished as* BRENDAN *and the* FATHER *approach from his left and right. They look at each other and then* EDDIE.)

BRENDAN: The bright-eyed eldest son she never stopped talking about. Home from London for the first time in a decade. The Smiler O'Rourke we always called him. He'd sell a rat's hole to a blind man for a wedding ring and still he'd be smiling at the end of it.

(BRENDAN *leans against the broken door-frame.*)

FATHER: Eight months it was empty before the video shop moved in. Eight months when I'd walk to the pub every Sunday evening and look in the bare window. There, among the dust and dismantled sheaves on the floor I could see that wallet she gave you on your twenty-first birthday. I always wanted to ask you did you lose it or just throw it there when you were leaving?

(EDDIE *looks at him but does not reply. The* FATHER *speaks to* BRENDAN *as he walks off.*)

FATHER: There are things you don't ask a man even when he is your own son.

(EDDIE *leans back against the other door-frame for a moment, staring ahead of him before* BRENDAN *slaps his head from behind, making* EDDIE *dart forward, startled.*)

BRENDAN: (*Amused*) Is this where they have you now, brother?

EDDIE: (*Defensively*) It's a job.

BRENDAN: Jaysus, a gochie in a hut. Are you keeping the punters out of the supermarket or holding them in?

EDDIE: Shopping trolleys. A lot of the women out here have no way of getting their messages home so they just go walkabout with the trolley. My job is to take it from them here at the gate.

BRENDAN: You call it a job, sitting like a toy soldier in this tin can of a hut?

EDDIE: It brings in more than the assistance. Three years of my life working in that shop, whatever hours under the sun and moon she asked me. They told me in the labour exchange. She never paid over a penny of my PRSI or PAYE these last eighteen months. Every morning she'd send me down to the cake shop for cream doughnuts while she made the coffee. 'Her treat,' she always called it (BRENDAN *laughs*), 'her treat for her favourite man.'

BRENDAN: How much?

EDDIE: What?

BRENDAN: More?

EDDIE: What?

BRENDAN: Than the assistance?

EDDIE: (*Shrugs his shoulders*) Six or seven pounds.

(BRENDAN *darts forward to slap him on the head again as* EDDIE *ducks and darts away from him.*)

BRENDAN: You're a gobshite, brother.

EDDIE: I'm sick of scraping around for something. You get tired of looking for the perfect job, the perfect anything. You lose hope, you lose the will to get up and look for something, to skimp for the bus fare to the interview, to find the nerve to face the row of suits quizzing you about your last employment, to feel guilt in your stomach no matter how hard you looked for work. So you just stay at home brooding, putting off getting up because you're in terror of the slitted brown envelopes waiting to trap you in the hall.

BRENDAN: Jaysus, what's to stop you getting out, even just sitting in the park?

EDDIE: I may as well be sitting here as sitting in the park. Trees aren't pretty when you're forced to look at them long enough: just twisted bark like dried-up lives. What else have I to do? You can't put two people and a child in a small house without a penny for twenty-four hours a day without them clawing each other's throats out.

BRENDAN: All right kid, I'm only slagging.

EDDIE: (*Sullenly*) It's easy to slag without a kid to feed, without her eyes glued to your pocket every time you walk in, hoping against hope you have a treat for her.

(BRENDAN *sits down on the wardrobe*.)

BRENDAN: Listen brother, you'd swear you were the first father in the history of the world. Would you look at the tension in your shoulders? You're only twenty-four for God's sake and you'd swear your life was over. Getting so screwed up about things isn't helping Eileen or the little monster.

(EDDIE *looks at him and pauses*.)

EDDIE: It's always been easier for you, Brendan. I don't know why, you've been able to swan through it, let nothing ever affect you. I tried but I've never been able to do that. I take everything more personal. If something is not right I think it's my fault, that I've failed if I can't make it perfect. Maybe it's how we were brought up.

BRENDAN: We never wanted for anything.

EDDIE: I don't mean that, I mean . . . after Mammy died, like there was an absence in the house that could never be filled, like we were never completely a family again. When I look at Orla I want things to be different, I want to relive those years again only through her this time with no sudden halt in the middle, with a mother and a father and bright clothes and food on the table.

(BRENDAN *is quiet for a moment*.)

BRENDAN: Old *Madame X*, eh, still gazing in the window. Don't think I don't remember too, but it was different for me. I was older, I understood more what her death really meant, I wasn't able to run away from it like you then. It hurt, you know, a numb ache for a long time. Nights I'd wake, just make out your white vest like a ghost across from me in the bed, crying silently so you would not be disturbed. We tried to cushion you from it, kid, but Christ how it hurt. Never let myself get caught like that again, ducking and weaving, never letting anything get too close to me.

(*There is a pause. Their eyes both shift across the stage.*)

EDDIE: (*Calls*) Sorry love, you'll have to leave that trolley at the gate.

(BRENDAN *laughs.*)

What?

BRENDAN: I always knew you were cut out for management.

(EDDIE *smiles ruefully, more at ease with himself.*)

EDDIE: Will you go up and see Eileen and the kid?

BRENDAN: I haven't time. I'm driving tonight.

EDDIE: Where to?

(BRENDAN *stands up on the wardrobe.*)

BRENDAN: The arse of France with four hundred birds. Have to be there for dawn the day after tomorrow. It's an amazing sight, kiddo – you never tire of it – the countdown on the beach at dawn. They know they're getting out, you can hear them squawking, flapping their wings up against the bars, their excitement getting through to your own bloodstream. You're waiting there, stopwatch in one hand, cigarette in the other and at seven fifteen you hit that lever and it's a sound like no other. Four hundred cages opening, four hundred pairs of wings spreading out. It's like a tornado in the desert, a solid mass of the softest down rising, scattering outwards and away. And you think of all the little terraces in Dublin, all the men getting up, the empty lofts silent on the roofs of the sheds, the time clocks and binoculars and the hours of patient waiting. Up there above you they're fanning out, buffeted by winds, casting shadows on the sea below. And some will die or lose their way but the rest will fly unnoticed, a speck above the heads of people who will never know the miracle of them finding their way home. It's a good feeling that, kid, standing on the beach with your work done, a big empty wagon full of bird shit and stray feathers and nothing left to do except turn and head for home.

EDDIE: You're a jammy bastard.

(BRENDAN *jumps down as if to hit him again and* EDDIE *darts away.*)

BRENDAN: And nothing at home to head for except the remains of the meal you had before you left and the clothes in a plastic bag from the launderette. You might say you would, but you wouldn't swap, kiddo. Here.

(*He reaches into his pocket and takes out a few banknotes.*)

EDDIE: (*Pushing his hand away*) I don't want your money.

BRENDAN: It's not for you. Get a teddy or a couple of gewgaws for the monster.

EDDIE: Why don't you give them to her yourself?

BRENDAN: If I brought them she wouldn't know they was from you.

(*He pushes the money into* EDDIE's *pocket, then shoves him with a friendly clatter across the stage towards where the* HORSE *has been kneeling.*)

Mind the flying trolleys, kiddo.

(*As* BRENDAN *retreats* EDDIE *stares at the* HORSE *who rises and begins to speak in a distant, little-girl voice as she drifts across the stage towards the ramp, at the top of which* MAUREEN *now appears.* EDDIE *follows the* HORSE *as if in a trance.*)

HORSE: Look at the bulbs in the trees jangling in the wind, Daddy. Look at all the lights in the sale in Clery's. Where is your hand, Daddy, where is your hand?

(*The* HORSE *sinks down at the foot of the ramp which* MAUREEN *has come down to stare at* EDDIE. EILEEN *comes between them and stops in front of* EDDIE.)

EILEEN: What are you doing here, Eddie?

EDDIE: Are you half-cracked, woman, dragging the child across town in the lashings of rain with them shoes on her?

EILEEN: What are you on about, Eddie, it's only a wee drop of rain?

(MAUREEN *sinks down to put her arm around the* HORSE.)

MAUREEN: My friend drove them. We called out and collected them.

(EDDIE *turns on her*.)

EDDIE: What have you got to do with the shoes my child wears? This is a family matter, between my wife and me.

EILEEN: Eddie, what's wrong? And how did you get here? I thought you were at work in the supermarket all day.

EDDIE: And this is where you bring the child to when I am out, is it? To a junkie's flat so she can stare at the puffed-up eyeballs of her favourite auntie?

EILEEN: Maureen's my sister, Eddie! The child needs to get away from those same four walls every day.

EDDIE: Away into this? A corporation flat that should have been condemned a decade ago? Can we at least not wait until she is a little bit older?

EILEEN: What's happened, Eddie? Why are you here?

(EDDIE *is silent for a moment, clenching and unclenching his fist*.)

EDDIE: A pound deposit.

EILEEN: What?

EDDIE: Per trolley. A schoolboy gives you a little ticket on the way in and a refund on the way out. The marketing people were over from London. They're worried about the image. A tin hut at the gate doesn't look smart enough.

EILEEN: They don't need you any more?

EDDIE: (*Bitterly*) They gave me a full day's pay for today.

(EDDIE *lowers his head, suddenly defeated-looking with all the anger drained from him. He holds his empty hand out as if offering it to her. Eileen takes it and rubs her forehead lightly against his, nuzzling up to him*.)

EILEEN: You did your best, Eddie. Never mind, it was just a few quid more than the dole. We managed before and we'll manage now. (*She moves back to look down at the* HORSE.) Orla will be glad to have her Daddy home to play with her again.

(MAUREEN *rises and sits on the wardrobe*.)

MAUREEN: A corporation flat that should have been con-demned years ago, eh? Mr Shagging Perfect, couldn't even mind a few shopping trolleys. Mr Mortgage on a house in Tallaght the size of an old-fashioned fridge. Mr Church Wedding, Mr Doing His Duty. Learn by my mistakes I should have told Eileen, have nothing to do with the righteous little fucker.

EDDIE: Our life has nothing to do with you.

EILEEN: The child's nappy is wet.

(EDDIE *moves forward towards the* HORSE.)

EDDIE: I'll change her for you.

(*He kneels beside the* HORSE.)

MAUREEN: At least my fellow had some hope of doing his duty. Gerard, eh, my own bank clerk with a face like a slapped arse and a life-long mistrust of zips. I was there before you, lover boy, a queen at seventeen, my own little house in the arse of Balbriggan. Jesus Christ, Balbriggan! Little town houses designed for gnomes, almost as small as the yoke you saddled my sister with. Ask your wife would she swap that box up in the hills for this flat. Go on, ask her.

EDDIE: (*Ignoring her*) She feels all hot. Christ, if she gets a temperature out of this kip.

EILEEN: Eddie, calm down. The child is fine.

MAUREEN: At least Gerard had a job before he started giving himself airs. God, they'll have a good snigger at you in the labour exchange tomorrow, lover boy. You could have just been a number, kept your head down and found something on the black. But no, you sign off for six weeks' Mickey Mouse work. They'll have all the forms waiting and the questions. You're marked out now, they'll be checking you so close you won't even hear them drop like owls swooping over a mouse.

EDDIE: Stay away from my daughter and my wife, junkie!

(MAUREEN *rises. We know that she has flinched inside. As she speaks she exits through the doorway and* EILEEN *moves up to the top of the ramp.*)

MAUREEN: (*A quieter, colder voice*) I can leave them in safe hands all right, with such a good provider.

(EDDIE *rises and begins to pace the stage, glancing anxiously towards* EILEEN *at the top of the ramp who turns to look down at him. The* HORSE *has risen and begun to circle him.*)

EILEEN: It's no good, Eddie, she can keep nothing down. It's the third time this evening.

EDDIE: (*Harassed, sharply*) I know, I know. Haven't I been carrying her around in my arms? I'm trying to think of something, there must be something . . .

EILEEN: Take it easy, Eddie. These things happen, it's not your fault. Maybe we should bring her down here. A new house shouldn't have mould like that in the bedrooms. God, her clothes stink.

EDDIE: I'll change her for you.

EILEEN: I've nothing dry to put on, unless we wrap her in one of your old shirts. I wasn't expecting it. She's been going through clothes all evening, even things she's long outgrown. It takes so long to wash them by hand.

EDDIE: (*Snaps*) Stop getting at me. If I could get you a washing machine I would!

EILEEN: (*Snaps back*) Who's getting at you? Who's asking you for one? Will you just go up and hold the child while I find something. She's whimpering up there, I'm sure she has that temperature back.

EDDIE: A doctor, she must have a doctor.

EILEEN: You think he'd come out here at this hour on a medical card? I'll take her down to the clinic in the morning. We'll sponge her down again.

EDDIE: Will she take nothing?

EILEEN: What is there to take? Hot milk and honey might make her sleep if we had honey. I suppose we could ask Carol next door again . . .

EDDIE: No.

EILEEN: Maybe . . .

EDDIE: (*Shouts*) No more maybes! I'm sick to death of maybes!

EILEEN: Eddie, will you calm down. Go up to her there, she's crying.

(*As* EDDIE *goes to the ramp the* HORSE *confronts him. He stops. The* OLD MAN *has appeared at the top of the ramp.*)

EDDIE: I can't.

EILEEN: What?

EDDIE: I can't face her. I'm ashamed, Eileen. It's my fault, no matter what you say, it's mine. She's ill now more often than she's well. I can't face her eyes empty-handed . . .

EILEEN: Eddie, please . . .

EDDIE: I'm going . . .

(*The* HORSE *moves from* EDDIE'S *path and he is confronted now by the* OLD MAN. EDDIE *backs away startled.* EILEEN *has withdrawn to the side of the stage.*)

OLD MAN: You came to me twice, boy, you should know my face by now . . .

EDDIE: Get to hell out of my head.

OLD MAN: . . . as well as I know every vein in your neck from when you held me down, know your eyes that were no longer human the second time you came. I have the right to haunt you, boy, because your face is all that haunts me now.

(*The* OLD MAN *moves past* EDDIE.)

EDDIE: You crazy old bastard. I never meant you harm, I just wanted . . .

(*The* OLD MAN *kneels beside the wardrobe, taking out a cloth and wiping its surface, with his back to* EDDIE.)

OLD MAN: I kept the bottom half of the house well, there's no one can say I did not. (*He looks up.*) The ceilings upstairs I couldn't reach those last years, damp patches blotching them, the white paint flaking away. (*He looks back down.*) But only the missus and I saw the shame of that, nobody else up those stairs for years, except the doctor and the young priest once a month, until that night . . .

(*The lighting has changed slightly as* EDDIE *darts forward, suddenly hunched down, alert.*)

EDDIE: (*Half-whisper, edge of fear in his voice*) Fuck it, I thought the gaff was empty. Listen here, old man, just take it easy, right. I didn't know you were in here.

(*The* OLD MAN *rises and looks towards him, a hand raised as if shielding his eyes from strong light.*)

OLD MAN: Who's that? What are you, a boy, a man? What do you want here?

EDDIE: I was looking for scrap, something I might be able to sell to get some money, I didn't know . . .

OLD MAN: Robbing! When I wanted money I worked for it, without a day sick for forty-eight years. I didn't get it by looting and stealing, you pup!

EDDIE: (*His nerves shattered with fear*) Right, listen, I thought this kip was abandoned, the place is falling down around your head. I thought I might find something. Now just shut up and let me get out of here.

(*The* OLD MAN *blocks his path as* EDDIE *turns to run.*)

OLD MAN: I should know how my own house looks. You know Cabra West, boy? All those estates of houses: Offaly Road, Newgrange Ave, all the streets down to Phibsborough? Who built them, eh? Tell me that? The church there with the green dome and the stone angel hovering over the door? Who built that then, eh? Tell me! Tell me!

EDDIE: I don't know. MacInerny or Belton, some rich bastard like that. (*Shouts*) Now just shut up and let me the hell out of here!

(*The* OLD MAN *draws himself erect to stare straight at* EDDIE.)

OLD MAN: I did. Me and a hundred men like me. Navvies, bricklayers, carpenters. Mixing cement with the hands numb from cold for the likes of you to live in them, you young coward. Come on then, you can't even take an old man on!

EDDIE: (*Backing away*) You keep your distance you old bastard or by God I'll floor you.

OLD MAN: (*Contemptuous*) Rooting among the leftovers of people's lives for 'something to sell for money', eh. For what? For drugs, is it, huh? So you can hang around crazed out of your head on some street corner.

EDDIE: For a sick child.

OLD MAN: (*Snorts*) A sick child! You have to hide behind a child to justify yourself. I don't believe you, boy. (*He spits.*) Now go to hell for your money!

(*The* OLD MAN *lunges across suddenly at* EDDIE *and as they tussle the* HORSE *emerges from the shadows behind them, speaking in the voice of a frail and slightly deranged old woman and freezing* EDDIE *and the* OLD MAN *locked together in combat. They break suddenly, both their faces filled with terror.*)

HORSE: Larry, is that our son Larry come home late? Larry?

OLD MAN: My wife, she's dotting. Good Jesus, boy, you'll kill her with the shock of it if she sees you.

EDDIE: Will you just let me go!

(EDDIE *pushes the* OLD MAN *who staggers back off-stage as* EDDIE *moves to the front of the stage with his hands over his ears, trying to drown out the* HORSE *who passes by his hunched back.*)

HORSE: Larry? Larry?

(*The* HORSE *abruptly ceases and* EDDIE *looks up, almost snarling with fear at the* HORSE *who now stands directly behind him.*)

EDDIE: No! (*Pause, as he looks around.*) Everything's gone white, so white. I want to fade into it. I want the smell of poppies. I want to forget, if only your voice would stop calling that name. Where are you?

HORSE: Can you not hear me whispering inside your veins?

EDDIE: Like waking between dreams. I'm so cold I'm frightened. I shouldn't feel this cold.

HORSE: You've forgotten the path home, son. Is it out along the canal or down through the estates? Children splashing in the Silver Spoon, ribs like rows of silvery needles.

EDDIE: When are we going home, Mammy?

HORSE: Soon, son. Very, very soon. Eileen will be waiting up for you all night, with your child wrapped in an old shirt asleep in her arms.

(EILEEN *comes to the doorway.* EDDIE *stares, frightened.*)

EDDIE: Like she's at the end of a tunnel. Like I could put my hand in and touch her.

HORSE: Can you not see, son? It's a trick glass.

(*The* HORSE *turns to look towards* EILEEN *who calls excitedly back towards* EDDIE.)

EILEEN: There's no doubts about it Eddie, it's on the six o'clock news. From the horse's own mouth, the Minister himself. An extra week's assistance for Christmas.

EDDIE: (*Coming to himself*) But only for people two hundred and ten unbroken days on the dole.

EILEEN: How long is it since that job at the supermarket?

EDDIE: What?

(EILEEN *leans as if examining an imaginary calendar on the wall.*)

EILEEN: The week after Orla's birthday, that's April, May, June . . . thirty days there, up to the 22nd. (*Pause, then she looks up.*) Eddie?

EDDIE: What?

EILEEN: Thanks be to Christ they sacked you when they did. (*Joyous*) You made it. By five days you scraped in.

EDDIE: I didn't?

(*She hugs him.*)

EILEEN: You did!

EDDIE: Jesus, I did something! (*He crosses over to lean on the other side of the doorway*.) A whole extra week's.

EILEEN: Food, chicken we can stuff on Christmas Day, maybe find a few second-hand clothes in the Simon shop. There's good bargains there like new. We'll have a fire and put both bars of that heater on out in the hall Christmas Day so the whole house will feel warm.

EDDIE: A present for Orla, a real one. She'll know it's Christmas this year, she's old enough.

EILEEN: I'd promised to take her into town . . . not buy anything, just to look at the shop windows, see the lights at dusk in the streets.

EDDIE: A present for her to open, not just bits of copying books and knick-knacks.

EILEEN: (*Allowing herself to dream*) Oh Eddie, imagine if we could buy her a bicycle (*the* HORSE *crosses the stage to stand for a moment between them, staring at* EDDIE *before exiting*

174

through the doorway), a pink one with stabilizers like that little girl was riding last Sunday in the park, but it would cost . . . God, more than every penny extra we'd get.

EDDIE: (*Defensive suddenly*) Why not? Why can't Orla have what any other little girl would have?

EILEEN: But your shoes, Eddie?

EDDIE: My shoes are my own business. I want to look into my daughter's eyes on Christmas morning and just for once not feel small.

(EILEEN *moves forward and leans down as though gazing through a window.*)

EILEEN: Look at the gnomes in the window, Orla, look at the reindeer ready to pull all the presents for Santa. I'll lift you up, love.

(*The* HORSE *appears beside* EDDIE *in the doorway.*)

HORSE: That warm feeling in your limbs, Eddie, standing in line in the dole queue, remembering the child's face upstairs on the big green bus, babbling away, drawing shapes in the mist on the window.

(EDDIE *steps forward and walks stiffly towards* EILEEN. *He stops.*)

EILEEN: (*A half-whisper*) She was jumping up and down so much she fell asleep in the end. (*Excited*) Did you get it?

EDDIE: (*Stern-faced*) I got it.

(EILEEN *looks at him, alerted by something in his voice.*)

EILEEN: Was it . . . dearer than we thought?

(EDDIE *clasps the box so tight his knuckles are turning white.*)

EDDIE: It was the price we said it was. I got it.

EILEEN: Eddie . . . ?

EDDIE: (*A hiss*) I'll get up Christmas morning like any other father. Not be ashamed to look at my child's face.

EILEEN: Eddie, you'll wake the child. She'll want to know what's in the box.

EDDIE: I'll tell her it's ice to make ice cubes, love. Ice in case we're not cold enough.

EILEEN: Eddie, what's happened? What's wrong?

EDDIE: Sundays are my own, love, my day of rest. I didn't

need to be ashamed on Sundays. I wasn't unemployed. They don't count as working days.

EILEEN: What are you saying to me, Eddie?

EDDIE: I'm tell you I bought it, love, like I promised I would.

EILEEN: No extra week's money?

EDDIE: I'll walk you to the bus stop, love. You bring the child home, I've only money left for the one fare.

EILEEN: But what about the week ahead?

EDDIE: (*Near scream*) I bought it. I kept my promise.

EILEEN: How will you get home?

EDDIE: I'll walk with this, I'll deliver it, I will be Santa Claus!

EILEEN: Then I'll walk with you Eddie, I'll carry the child in my arms. You kept your promise Eddie, you were right. We'll manage someway. I love you, Eddie, I'll walk beside you . . . anywhere and for as long as it takes.

(*They turn and walk a few steps, framed by the light into a motionless silhouette. A pale light comes on the* HORSE.)

HORSE: I was watching over you, Eddie, every step of those thirteen miles home. The rain like a Chinese torture on your skull, the wet seeping through the plastic bags between your socks and leaking shoes. I was the Perpetual Star, framed by wire mesh every fifty paces along the motorway. I was the Christmas candle that you would set in the window to light Joseph's path. I was the words you never spoke. I was the longing that never left you, that you could never articulate. I was the hole in your heart, the dream you could never remember when you woke. I was that which could make you complete again. I was the space where God once lay on your tongue, the light of the sanctuary lamp that shimmered like a tear-drop turned upside-down. And I would glimmer in the street lights left on in the gritty daylight when you would walk every step of those thirteen miles again on Christmas morning.

(*The lights have come back up on* EDDIE *and* EILEEN *who walk forward a few paces, then stop.*)

EDDIE: Our child will taste turkey and ham for her Christmas dinner.

EILEEN: My sister will feed us, Eddie.

EDDIE: I'll not bring my daughter to a junkie.

EILEEN: (*Hurt*) You'd sooner have her sit with every tramp and knacker who's been sleeping rough on the city streets.

EDDIE: We'll have our Christmas dinner served to us in the Mansion House.

EILEEN: Charity! And every politician down for five minutes to have their photograph taken with us?

EDDIE: And when the first one of them tries to shake my hand . . .

EILEEN: You can take up your knife, Eddie, and drive it through his heart.

(*She walks on and he follows her off-stage.*)

ACT TWO

The stage begins in darkness. There is the noise of a car crash off-stage built into the music before the lights gradually come up to reveal EDDIE *lying in a semi-sleeping state on the wardrobe with the* HORSE *watching over him motionless at the top of the ramp.* BRENDAN *enters and walks to the edge of the wardrobe. He looks at* EDDIE *and* EDDIE *falls off on to the floor, waking and exchanging a dazed look with* BRENDAN *who backs away into the corner.* EILEEN *has come on to the stage and stands in the other corner.* EDDIE *looks towards the* HORSE *who is slowly descending the ramp.*

HORSE: The noise of the crash, Eddie, waking you in your dinky house, the faded coverlet falling from your shoulders, the worn carpet itching for the soles of your feet. Did you even think of your brother, did you?

EDDIE: I thought of Orla, even in my sleep, Orla.

HORSE: Was it in a dream or had you really heard it? The noise so close like it happened in the room next door.

(EDDIE *stands up on the wardrobe.*)

EDDIE: In Orla's room. I woke and I cried 'Orla!' I was dreaming. She was saying things that I couldn't hear or couldn't understand the language, and her eyes . . . never looking up with the shame and we were in the centre of the road by the Gresham suddenly and still she wouldn't look up or take my hand no matter how much I shouted to warn her, veering off into the path of the cars, trucks barely missing her. And then she was falling, falling into the traffic and I heard a

crash and a scream in a voice I knew and I woke with a thud
like the heart was pulled out of me.

(*They look at each other with sudden instinctive fear before*
EILEEN *attempts to control the situation.*)

EILEEN: You're making me jumpy, Eddie. It was a dream.
The child is safe, let her sleep. You can't be watching over
her night and day.

(EDDIE *goes down on to his knees as* EILEEN *backs away
into the shadows.*)

HORSE: That noise so close, Eddie, that noise so close . . .

(EDDIE *has looked towards the* HORSE *and not noticed the*
FATHER *coming to stand behind him.*)

FATHER: Eddie, can you hear? I woke in the middle of the
night, the radio policeman's motorbike crackling along the
street. Eddie, can you hear me?

EDDIE: No, I don't want to hear.

(EDDIE *turns as the* FATHER *speaks.*)

FATHER: The Spanish authorities had problems identifying
him, they said, the front wheel of the truck still spinning,
a confetti of pale feathers littering the roadway. That
small bit of money I'd been saving for the holiday I
promised your mother before she died, Eddie. Almost two
decades sitting in the bank like a weight on my soul that I
was unable to bring myself to touch. It was meant for Orla
when I died. Five days he had been lying there, son. Five
glasses of orange juice on the locker beside his bed, five
bent straws collecting a film of dust. Five stale bread rolls
for five breakfasts beside them. Five days' stubble on his
chin and five days of filth which he was lying in. Do you
understand me, Eddie? The hospital attendants' job was
to bring your brother his breakfast, not to feed it to him.
Bound hand and foot like Christ on the cross, staring at
the orange juice all day, fantasizing that the glass was
glowing at night. The skin all blotched and broken on his
buttocks. I knew that I was hurting him, almost having to
scrape the dried-in faeces off. I was his father. You think
I would have screamed at the hospital staff, but they just

shrugged and kept their distance. The little doctor muttering in broken English (*broken English*) 'The truck it hits the wall, blood test, airport, Aids.'

HORSE: Brendan. You wore his clothes, Eddie, his football boots when he outgrew them. Half the neighbours even called you Brendan, as if you were shrunk back to size again. Shielded you when your mother died, introduced you to cigarettes in the lane behind the house, to drink when your Da was out, let you play spin-the-bottle when you were just eleven and the girls all fifteen.

FATHER: When are you going in to see him, Eddie? (*Suddenly angry*) The man is your brother.

(*In backing away* EDDIE *has reached* BRENDAN *who suddenly grabs his hand from behind and twists it around so that* EDDIE *is facing him.*)

BRENDAN: How could you sleep with a thirst like that, kiddo, your body crying out, not knowing if anyone would ever come? With a sandpaper throat and a stomach sickened from my own stench, praying like Christ in the desert for one drop of moisture. Only word of English anyone ever spoke to me in that hospital was 'Insurance. Insurance.' Only face I kept seeing was this lovely Dutch girl I gave a lift to in France, looked just seventeen. Staggered up into the cab like she was moving in slow motion, talking away to herself. Sat in beside me and fell asleep with her head on my shoulder as I drove. The smile she had while the night turned dark on the motorway, the way the shadows slid over her face as we sped under the street lights. We shared a needle back in her squat. That's the joke, Eddie. I'll never know what gave it to me. Was it the needle or the fuck? At least the truck was empty, the pigeons flying through the rain back to Neilstown and Tallaght and the Broadstone.

(EDDIE *backs away from him, holding the hand stiffly that* BRENDAN *has touched.*)

HORSE: What were you but a failed version of him?

EDDIE: (*Backing away*) A father. That's what I was. A father . . .

HORSE: What sort of father tries to kill his own child?

EDDIE: No! I was her father! I loved her. I wanted to protect her, to save her from . . . I never . . .

HORSE: It was yourself you were thinking of with the burden of Orla lifted from your shoulders, no thoughts, no responsibility.

EDDIE: It's not true. I would never have done it. I was deranged from grief. It was just talk, talk . . .

HORSE: Don't try to hide from me, Eddie. I know every twist of your mind. I was the void waiting inside your heart that you were terrified to fill.

EDDIE: Orla! Everything that I lived for.

FATHER: (*Firmly*) He is your brother.

(*The* FATHER *walks back and* EDDIE *turns to see* EILEEN, *who has emerged behind him.* EDDIE *looks down at his right palm which he is rubbing with his left hand, then looks up at her again.*)

EILEEN: How was he?

EDDIE: Didn't know what to do at the end of the visit. I clasped my hand over his, only his fingers visible above the plaster, and even as he tried to squeeze it I knew what I was going to do. I hated myself but I knew. All the way down the hospital corridor holding my hand out like it wasn't part of me any longer. All the way I kept thinking: it's not me that will get it, somehow I'll give the disease to Orla. Stopping at the jakes, making myself not go in. But I was only delaying the moment. Even on the bus I held my hand out stiffly, finally getting off in the middle of nowhere and almost running into the toilet in the nearest pub to scald the hand off myself with hot water. I scrubbed it dry on a filthy towel, knowing I was betraying him, that I had more chance of catching something off the towel than my brother, but I was shaking, I couldn't control the fear. (*He looks down.*) Aids. Aids. I still can't, it's like my hand that touched him will never be clean again.

(BRENDAN *approaches* EDDIE *from the back and puts his hand on his shoulder. The* HORSE *sits on the wardrobe.*)

BRENDAN: Eddie. Come on, I've the truck outside. I'm going

up to the breaker's yard. Are you coming for the spin?
Bring the little monster.

(EDDIE *joins him, holding an imaginary child in his arms,
and they walk a few paces before stopping.* EDDIE *looks
behind him as* BRENDAN *stares ahead.*)

BRENDAN: A good wing-mirror here if I can just find it
among the junk. An amazing gaff, this. Half a century
here. Remembers it all, Joey does. Jaysus, the guy is so
cute he probably remembers going to a dance with his
father and coming home with his mother.

(EDDIE *goes to stand behind the* HORSE *with his hand on
her shoulder.*)

EDDIE: The gee-gees, Orla, look at the gee-gees . . .

(BRENDAN *turns and follows his gaze.*)

The two lovely white foals after coming into the yard,
Orla. Do you . . . ? (*His expression grows puzzled as he turns
to look at* BRENDAN.) What are they at, Brendan, wandering around the parked cars? God they're almost staggering.

BRENDAN: Can you not see what they're doing, kiddo? Joey
the breaker told me about it. Look at the way they put
their nostrils right down out of sight, the way that foal is
stumbling against the side of the van.

EDDIE: What are they doing, what?

BRENDAN: They come down the carriageway and get in here
where there are parked cars. They're sniffing the petrol
caps, they're getting stoned.

EDDIE: (*Moving back a few paces*) I don't believe you.

BRENDAN: Watch it with your own eyes, kiddo. Look around
you, show me one blade of grass. Even the horses need to
be stoned to survive here.

EDDIE: Everyone except you, big brother, eh . . . ?

(BRENDAN *exits.* EDDIE *watches and then follows him to
the doorway where the* FATHER *enters. They exchange a
look as* EILEEN *comes to stand at the other side of the*
FATHER. *The* FATHER *moves forward and stops, looking
down as though addressing the ground.* EILEEN *and* EDDIE
move back, allowing him privacy as he blesses himself.)

FATHER: Every week I used to come here once, Mary. Lemonade bottle filled with water, a few flowers from the old lady outside the gate. Haven't been so often lately, you don't grow out of grief, but ... it just upsets me too much. Always wondered would the two boys ever come when I join you here. The wood of my coffin merging with the wood of yours over the decades until there would be nothing between us ever again. Remember, Mary, that freezing winter the year after Brendan was born. The cold he got from it, three weeks lying between us in the bed, his hot little forehead, his cries every ten minutes when the cough woke him again. It was so exhausting getting up to face work every morning but I loved those nights most of all, waking to feel him there with you and me on both sides, protecting him from all harm. That's the way it will be now Mary, for the length of eternity, the wood of his coffin between us, his Mammy and Daddy on both sides. Seven stone two this morning when he died. The first grey hint of dawn and him lying so still for hours that except for the blimp of the machine you'd swear he was gone. I had carried him up the stairs on my back when he was last that weight. I had carried ... (*Pause.*) Oh my dead wife, will you ever forgive me for failing you with our son. And even if you do, my love, will I ever forgive myself?

(*The* FATHER *blesses himself, then turns his head, changing the mood, and looks towards* EDDIE.)

Things to do, son. If there weren't things to do we'd all go to pieces. The undertaker needs the wording for the papers.

(EDDIE *looks at him.*)

EDDIE: He was a junkie, Da. From the moment he put that needle in his arm he was just dead meat lumbering around.

FATHER: We'll tell them your brother died from injuries in the crash.

(*The* FATHER *exits and* EDDIE *crosses the back of the stage. He finds an old battered teddy bear which he kicks at idly for a moment then picks up. He sits down next to the ramp holding the teddy, frozen in the posture of a man who has been rocking back and forth. He holds this still pose until* EILEEN *appears on the far side of the stage. The* HORSE *has sunk down into the child-like posture at the front of the stage, with her arm covering her face.*)

EILEEN: You can't just sit here upstairs all night with the light out, Eddie. (*He doesn't acknowledge her.*) At least get off the floor and into the bed . . . or try to pretend that you even notice I am here.

EDDIE: Why?

EILEEN: Eddie . . .

EDDIE: The whole city's doing smack but not him. I can't understand it. OK, you see kids hanging round street corners with their eyes glazed like slaughtered sheep piled up on a truck. But Brendan, he was too smart to be pumping shite into his arm. 'Light a cigarette, kiddo,' he said, 'and put it to my lips. Fuck the doctors, there's nothing they can do now.' I wanted to say 'Fuck you too, brother, fuck the whole lot of us.' All my life looking up to him, trying to fill the footsteps he left behind.

EILEEN: Come on downstairs, Eddie. You're not helping yourself or him or any of us brooding up here.

EDDIE: (*Rises*) Claimed he was never hooked, that he could have beaten the smack but just had to try it first. I'm not clever like Brendan was. I'm slow and awkward but I know when someone's lying. Why? Why?

EILEEN: People's lives, Eddie . . . I don't know why . . . sometimes they tilt off the edge. Could be any reason or none. Take my sister.

EDDIE: (*Almost sharply*) Your sister's different, she's just a . . .

EILEEN: (*Hurt*) A what?

EDDIE: (*Trying to withdraw*) Well I mean . . . I mean what has she got to live for?

EILEEN: And so what have you and I got to live for? (*Hurriedly*) Eddie, I didn't mean that, I . . .

(EDDIE *turns to look at her.*)

EDDIE: All those nights two years back when Orla cried out,

184

her bottom raw for want of Caldesene powder or Vasogen. Scraping my finger round to try and find the last bits of Sudocrem we'd been skimping with for a week, almost in tears when she was wet and we were trying to make the box of nappies last till dole day. Can you imagine how that felt for me, can you?

EILEEN: I'm the child's mother, Eddie, for God's sake.

EDDIE: And you're a good mother for her, making a home for her, making things last. But what sort of father stands around all day, watching his daughter in faded hand-me-downs whining because she has not had enough for her tea.

EILEEN: Eddie, you've got to face the fact that you've done your best for her. When did you last eat a full meal in this house? Almost shouting at me if I even buy you a new pair of socks, walking about in the rain in those pathetic shoes. Every penny goes on her . . .

EDDIE: But it's not enough is it? Not like my father and his father. I've still failed her as a father no matter what. And it's only beginning. I don't know what to do, how to protect her. I hear things, you know, I walk round these estates and I listen. The lollipop woman at the zebra crossing near the school?

EILEEN: The little woman? What about her?

EDDIE: The police have taken her away. She was passing out free samples of heroin from the pockets of her white coat to the kids starting in secondary school. The ice-cream van that used to park down by the green?

EILEEN: Eddie, I know all this happens. I don't want to hear about it.

EDDIE: He was paying her for the custom, they were flocking to him after school. The retired man who helped with the milk float? Couriering things in and out for his grandson to push them. That old house the County Council are always threatening to knock down? I heard them talking when I went in to use the jakes in the pub, anything you wanted, twelve- to fifteen-year-olds, boys, girls, hand jobs, blow jobs, straight fucks . . .

EILEEN: (*Distressed*) Stupid dirty talk from stupid sick men.

EDDIE: Anything, they said, anything . . .

EILEEN: What about all the ordinary people here getting on with ordinary lives, the likes of you and me . . .

EDDIE: Anything, they said, anything . . .

EILEEN: Eddie stop this! (*Almost sobbing*) And even if it happens, then that's the world outside our house. Keep it there, there's no need to drag it in here.

EDDIE: And we've brought a child into that world, with her battered teddy bear and the white bars of the cot she's long outgrown. How long more will that innocence last? I'm frightened for her, more frightened than by anything else.

(*He looks at the teddy in his hands and sinks down beside the* HORSE.)

A pillow and just a few seconds of struggle. She wouldn't wake, wouldn't even know what was happening to her. (*He looks towards* EILEEN.) I'd do the time for it gladly, Eileen, I'd take all the blame.

(*She screams and grabs the teddy from him suddenly as if about to claw at him with her nails.*)

EILEEN: Eddie, you bastard, bastard! Leave my child alone! Leave her . . .

(*The* HORSE *looks up at* EDDIE's *grief-stricken face as* EILEEN *backs away until she is at the entrance. The* HORSE *rises, towering over* EDDIE *who is on his knees. He looks up.*)

EDDIE: I never called to you that night.

HORSE: Your soul was crying out for me in anguish, your need aching to be filled.

EDDIE: I was half-crazed with grief at my brother's death.

HORSE: You were praying for anything that would halt the thoughts in your head.

EDDIE: You haunted my sleep, gnawing inside me like a germ.

HORSE: The child crying in the next room, the morning crawling past like a slug. What was your life but a radio left on between stations, a hiss of static nobody was listening to?

EDDIE: I was still young. I could have found work ...
hope ...

HORSE: You met the ghost of yourself at every age to come,
different shades of grey shuffling in and out of the labour
exchange.

EDDIE: All my life I just tried to do what was right.

HORSE: You took the kit off that boy in the park for yourself.

EDDIE: No, he was just a kid. I took it off him to save him. He
was straight. It was a sample somebody had handed him
from a car.

(*The* HORSE *has been circling him. Now she stands on the
wardrobe.*)

HORSE: There is no need to lie to me. It happens, Eddie, even
when you love your wife. You find yourself at a dance
some night, you meet a young girl and it's like you've
known all your life that you would meet her. All the
doubts you've ever had, the mornings you swore you
could not face another monotonous married day, the
reasons you clung on, duty, guilt, selflessness, fear. This
time you know you must think only of yourself. Her smile
jerks and freezes in the strobe lights on the dance floor.
She is waiting, Eddie.

(*She kneels on the wardrobe as though sexually beckoning him.*)
Oh, Eddie, my lover.

(EDDIE *kneels beside the wardrobe and the* HORSE *draws
him into an embrace.* EILEEN *suddenly pounds on the wood
of the doorway.*)

EILEEN: Eddie, Orla's in tears downstairs. She says you won't
open the bathroom door for her. Eddie, are you in there,
Eddie?

(*The* HORSE *puts a hand out to touch his cheek and draws
his own hand up to touch her neck.*)

HORSE: Now there's just you and me Eddie and the feel of
your skin all tense and waiting. Let me in, Eddie, let me
in to every inch of you. I am white and powdery on the
outside but within I am burning with passion in all the
colours that you could never name.

EDDIE: I don't want this, I don't know how I came to be here.

HORSE: Adultery is in your head and nothing will send it away. 'Get this, solve that, feed us, provide for us . . .' You've had enough of her, Eddie. You want me now, I who have no demands. Your body aching to forget these nothing years. Remember how you felt when you were eighteen?

EDDIE: I feared nobody then, nothing.

HORSE: You spat in the world's face. You thought it was your brother I fancied, but it was you, Eddie, you that I wanted to bring me home. Eddie, I'm still waiting, but what has happened to you since?

EDDIE: A child changes you, life is different.

EILEEN: (*Banging again, her voice anxious*) Eddie, are you all right in there?

(EDDIE *glances towards her voice, but the* HORSE *draws his attention back.*)

HORSE: That's what's happened to you, Eddie. 'The dishes, the kitchen, the kitchen, the dishes . . .' Scared of your own shadow here in this little Noddyland house.

EILEEN: (*Banging*) Eddie, can you not hear Orla calling you?

(EDDIE *turns his head again, startled by her voice.*)

EDDIE: (*Gruffly*) Go away!

HORSE: The little Daddy, eh? Your brother was a real man, Eddie, could fill me up, take me over. It was a joy to sleep with him.

(EDDIE *turns on his knees and grabs the bag from beside the wardrobe, confused and frightened, unable to make his mind up. The* HORSE *jumps down to confront him.*)

HORSE: The powder would flush in the toilet but not the needle, Eddie. How you would explain that to little wifey, eh, how would you talk your way out of this? It's time to stop thinking, Eddie. You just want me now, to taste my kiss this once, this only perfect time.

EILEEN: (*Panicking as she bangs for the last time*) Eddie, for Jesus' sake, open the door!

HORSE: Your face looks so old, but I'll make you young and strong again.

(*The* HORSE *spreads her arms out and closes them over his head, covering his body with the folds of the cloth. The* HORSE *retreats back as* EILEEN *approaches and looks at* EDDIE *sprawled on top of the wardrobe.* EDDIE *turns his head.*)

EDDIE: The pain doesn't hurt any more, Eileen.

EILEEN: Oh Jesus Christ, Eddie, you coward, you bastarding coward!

EDDIE: No Eileen, I want it to make it like it was before. Remember, Eileen . . .

(EILEEN *begins to back away and* EDDIE *slowly lumbers to his feet, putting his hand out towards her.*)

EDDIE: Eileen . . .

(EILEEN *stops and then climbs up on to the wardrobe and looks around her.*)

EILEEN: (*Excited*) Oh Eddie, Eddie! It's a beautiful little house. I never thought we'd have our own place so soon. (*Less certain*) We won't even notice the distance from the city.

EDDIE: It's for you, Eileen, a new start, make up for mistakes.

EILEEN: Will it be a boy or a girl I wonder? I won't know what coloured curtains to put up in its room.

EDDIE: We'll call her Orla if it's a girl. A new name in either family, a new start for us all.

EILEEN: You're a good man, Eddie. I mean it. Different from anyone else. Deep down I feel so safe with you.

EDDIE: (*Embarrassed but pleased*) I'm just myself, trying to do what's best for us.

(*They pause, staring at each other as the* FATHER *comes to stand behind* EDDIE.)

FATHER: One son abroad half the time and the other might as well have been. I took a bus from the Quays that seemed to take an eternity to reach its destination. Roofs of houses like seabirds on a cliff rising up to beyond where the eye could travel. 'The terminus,' the driver finally shouted. A stretch of half-finished carriageway, lights coming on in caravans. Milk churns and car tyres and bits of old washing machines. A boy of three naked from the waist down with a piece of stick in his hand. 'Not a bad estate,' he had said, 'just looks rough from the roadway in.'

EILEEN: It's your father, Eddie.

EDDIE: What?

FATHER: I felt like I was walking along the edge of nowhere. Not a car passing, not a person, just the upturned ghosts of cars across abandoned fields, stacks of doors and wing-mirrors, walking beyond the last street lamp carrying a christening shawl for my first granddaughter.

(*The* FATHER *walks back to the doorway.*)

EILEEN: Your father, Eddie, trying to read the numbers of the houses.

(EDDIE *turns and walks towards him excitedly.*)

EDDIE: Da! Da! You found us. (*Puzzled*) Can you not see me?

(*He searches his* FATHER'S *face as his* FATHER *looks through him.* EILEEN *has moved away and the* HORSE *walks to stand behind* EDDIE *almost touching him.*)

HORSE: I have stilled your body. But even I cannot control your dreams.

(*The* FATHER *blinks as though wakened from sleep.* EDDIE *shivers.*)

FATHER: Is that you, son, calling in the middle of the night?

EDDIE: I need money, Da, I need it bad.

FATHER: The child? Is Orla sick? Where's Eileen.

EDDIE: I just need money, Da. I must have cash.

(*The* FATHER *steps forward to observe him more closely.*)

FATHER: You look like shit, like death warmed up. Show me your eyes.

EDDIE: Ten pounds, twenty, Da. I need cash bad.

FATHER: What little money I had saved was spent getting your brother home from Spain, whatever was left I spent burying him. You never changed, did you, never grew up?

EDDIE: Dad . . .

FATHER: If your brother played cowboys, you'd play cowboys. If he jumped in the Liffey you'd jump in after him. (*Roars*) You fucking eegit, can't I see it written in your face?

EDDIE: You must have something left for me, your other son?

FATHER: There's only room in that grave for three. It's all I have left ahead of me and you'll not cheat me from lying with your mother. Die somewhere else if you are going to, but you'll not kill yourself on my doorstep.

(EDDIE *sinks down before the anger in his* FATHER'*s voice as the* FATHER *steps back and exits. The* HORSE *kneels beside him and takes his hand suddenly. He looks across, startled at her. The* HORSE *speaks in a little girl's voice.*)

HORSE: Daddy, why are you just sitting up here? Mammy's crying in the kitchen. She won't look up. Will you not tell me a bedtime story?

(EDDIE *smiles and she takes his hand, leaning against him as they kneel there.*)

EDDIE: What sort of story, Orla?

HORSE: One with a happy ending, in a place a long way from here.

EDDIE: You know all the stories, pick one.

HORSE: No, you tell me.

EDDIE: (*Thinks*) Once upon a time, a lifetime ago and a long way from here, there was a boy who had lost his Mammy. And because he could not cry or even say that word he found he had lost the power to speak. 'Mmmmm, muuuuhh,' was all he could say when he wanted to tell the people around him how he loved them.

HORSE: I don't like this story, Daddy, it's too sad.

EDDIE: Near where he lived there was a pool in the river called the Silver Spoon. And a few trees growing sideways up the slope of a hill. And sometimes when he went there he thought that he could see the flashing mane of a white horse, a mare as white as the soul of a little girl through the trees above him. Soon he began to feel that the mare was watching over him, that if he could only stay awake at night she would come and neigh beneath his window.

HORSE: What would the horse do, Daddy?

EDDIE: If the boy climbed down on to the shed roof and on to her back the white horse would bolt off and carry him away. And he would see his mother again riding in the sky and be able to sing words he never knew how to say, riding above the streets until dawn when he would wake in his bed as though nothing had happened with only a white strand of her mane like a silvery vein running across his palm.

HORSE: You're so quiet when you sit downstairs for hours as if you can't see me that I do be getting scared. Do you have secrets, Daddy?

(EDDIE *smiles and strokes her hair.*)

EDDIE: No secrets from you, my love.

HORSE: Then I'll have none for you, though Mammy told me not to say. There's eleven pounds and thirteen pennies in the dolls' box under my bed. All the money people gave me this year. When I have eleven pounds ninety-nine I can buy the Sindy doll in Super Crazy Prices. (*She kisses him.*) Good night, Daddy. I love you, though I didn't like your story much.

(*The* HORSE *rises and immediately turns back into the watching figure of the* HORSE *as she walks backwards towards the ramp.* EDDIE's *shoulders are stiff, he is visibly struggling with himself as he glances furtively over his shoulder, clenches his fists, and goes to kneel beside the ramp, groping under it until he produces a child's money box. He finds a child's T-shirt, wraps the money box in it and goes to kneel beside the wardrobe with the* HORSE *following him and lingering at his shoulder. He grimaces and holding the T-shirt up above his head with both hands smashes it down on to the stage with a cry, shattering open the money box inside. He opens the T-shirt and takes the coins from inside. As he rises the* HORSE *takes his hand and leads him back as* EILEEN *moves forward and kneels to look at* EDDIE.)

EILEEN: Never thought I could leave you, Eddie. I hate this place you brought me to, the silence of it in the morning when all the kids are at school. I hate the Hiace vans selling bad meat or stolen firewood. But it was home with you, our own place where our child could lay her head.

Bits of coloured drawings from magazines pinned above her cot, saucepans on the floor the only toys for her to play with. I loved the way you'd nuzzle up to me in your sleep for warmth, your patience when we had no money to buy condoms.

(*She picks up for a moment the T-shirt with the pieces of pottery inside it.*)

Eleven pounds and thirteen pennies. I heard the front door slam and ran upstairs. There were just bits of cheap pottery on the lino, shattered apart like my soul. (*She goes to ramp and calls softly.*) 'Orla! Get dressed, we're going to your Auntie Maureen's. Bold men came and stole your money box. Daddy has chased after them into the night. Your Auntie Maureen has sweets for you and lemonade.'

(EILEEN *exits. The* HORSE *moves back. There is a tussle of hands as* EDDIE *tries to hold on to her but she breaks free of him and steps back to watch from the front corner.* EDDIE *moves violently across the stage. He kicks the wardrobe and the frame of the door, causing* EILEEN *to appear at it.*)

EDDIE: That bitch Maureen. Of all the places you could bring her. Sleeping on a mattress on the floor, never knowing when the police will raid her.

EILEEN: Let her see whatever of life she will see there, but let her not see it from her own father.

EDDIE: (*Screams*) She's my child. All I have to live for. I want to see her!

(*He goes to dart towards the door but is stopped by* EILEEN'*s words.*)

EILEEN: I told her you were gone away, Eddie. Let her at least remember you as you were.

EDDIE: (*Almost a sob*) I didn't want to take her money. Can't you see that, after everything I've tried to give the child. (*He lifts his arm.*) I would cut this hand off and give it to her if she could only use it as a toy.

EILEEN: I'm sorry, Eddie. But stay away from me and my child. (EILEEN *steps back.* EDDIE *is left addressing the broken door-way.*)

EDDIE: Jesus, Eileen, I couldn't help it . . .

(*He turns to address the* HORSE *who steps further back from him.* EDDIE *does not see the* SHERIFF *come on stage.*)

EDDIE: The fire in my body, that same old ache that just had to be filled. Oh Christ, how I would welcome hell.

SHERIFF: Keogh? Eddie Keogh? The front door was open.

(EDDIE *turns, confused by where the voice is coming from.*)

SHERIFF: We've written to you, Mr Keogh. You know what we're here for. I'm sorry, but you were the foolish man not even to write back and make some offer on the arrears. The whole thing is to keep your file moving. Even a fiver a month. I have the repossession order here if you want to inspect it.

(*He approaches and tries to give* EDDIE *a piece of paper.* EDDIE *doesn't speak or look back at him. The* SHERIFF *puts the paper into* EDDIE's *limp hand and it falls to the ground. The* SHERIFF *glances around.*)

SHERIFF: Most people do a sort of runner before we arrive. They take, well, the smaller or more personal items, store them somewhere. I have to take everything that's here, you know that? Listen, maybe you didn't know the time we were due at. We're all family men ourselves. Do you want us to . . . have a smoke out the front, turn our backs for five minutes. You could pack a suitcase even. God knows, you'll need something.

EDDIE: A cigarette.

(*The* SHERIFF *steps forward, reaching into his pocket. He takes a cigarette packet out and flicks it open.*)

SHERIFF: Here, there's only three left. Keep the packet. Go on. Take something. We'll turn a blind eye.

(*He hands it to* EDDIE *who opens it, takes the cigarettes out and stuffs them in his pocket. He reaches out and picks up a few pieces of the shattered money box and places them in the packet which he carefully places into his pocket. He rises.*)

SHERIFF: Is that it? Everything you want?

(EDDIE *laughs manically to himself at the question as the* SHERIFF *exits.* EDDIE *moves to sit on the edge of the wardrobe, his head sunk in despair. The* TRAMP *trots on to the stage in a jumpy state of extreme agitation.*)

TRAMP: Here. This car is taken. House rules. You want to sleep in it you bring your own bottle like the rest of us.

EDDIE: (*Thick mutter*) Leave me alone.

(*He tries to shake off the man's hand as the* TRAMP *grips his shoulder but the* TRAMP *grips him tighter.*)

TRAMP: You're not listening, pal. Now you can kip in them oul wrecks of yokes the cream-crackers have torn asunder beyond by the canal, but you're not coming into my car in my laneway without your own bottle. I hate people who bum drink.

EDDIE: I don't drink.

(*The* TRAMP *steps back to peer at him and laughs.*)

TRAMP: Too good for it are you? Nothing but the best for you, fill yourself up to the eyeballs with shit.

EDDIE: It's raining, I'm sleeping in this shagging car!

(*The* TRAMP *grabs him and lifts him up, moving over to fling him down on to the ramp. He spits down on* EDDIE *then steps back to sit on the wardrobe.*)

TRAMP: I could be your grandda, pal, and still you're only like a feather to me. You won't last a month on the street. You don't just walk into a car like this, you've to work for it. Where do you think you are, Butlin's? I'd to split a Corkman's head open with a rock for it. There's a skip around the corner for the likes of you, there's gutters. A car like this, it's an investment, a home from home. And you'll not even get into it with VP Sherry. Spirits, shorts, no meths here. And no bottle, no warmth. Get your own car.

(EDDIE *lies sprawled on the ramp as the* TRAMP *walks off.*)

EDDIE: So fucking cold suddenly. Brendan, haunt me, haunt me! I'll not be scared, you can come out! Mother, Christ how many years have I hated that word. Anyone, anything. Don't leave me down here to die alone in the pissings of rain. All I ever wanted was just to fill this hole in my heart, to belong, not to be haunted by this unease.

(*The* HORSE *holds out her hands on the far side of the stage, as though pleading with him.*)

HORSE: 'Man and wife,' the priest said, Eddie, and you believed him. And she's left you here. But I haven't left you, Eddie, it's you that's letting me drain away. Going down these back lanes, not taking me with you. But I don't bear grudges. I'm waiting to come for you again. Inside I'm all a-tremble to be your bride.

(EDDIE *half-rises and looks towards her.*)

EDDIE: Who are you? (*Shouts*) I have to know. (*Pause.*) Are you the ghost of my mother?

HORSE: I am the ghost of all dreams.

EDDIE: (*Pleading*) Then fill this ache in my soul . . .

HORSE: I'll be waiting, son. The waste ground by the Silver Spoon. I'll be there when you have fallen, beyond the lights of tinkers' caravans by the stream where you used to play.

EDDIE: I'm growing so cold, so cold.

HORSE: (*Turning abruptly with a click of her fingers*) Find the money first, boy. My warmth doesn't come cheap!

(EDDIE *rises and staggers towards the doorway.* MAUREEN *comes out to face him.*)

MAUREEN: You're keeping late hours, lover boy. Don't often get the pleasure of a visit from you. They're not here.

EDDIE: Smack, I need some smack, I need it now.

(*She turns and walks on-stage with* EDDIE *following her.*)

MAUREEN: The cool, clean lover who didn't even want his daughter visiting here?

EDDIE: Smack, I've lost my works, everything. This time of night I don't know where to get it over here. Just tell me where to go. Tell me.

MAUREEN: You looked down your nose at me long enough. Now I'm not ashamed of what I am, but I'm not a pusher.

EDDIE: You have stuff here for yourself, I know you have.

MAUREEN: I'm cleaned out. I've nothing here.

EDDIE: I'll get you money tomorrow, I will.

MAUREEN: You failed at everything else. You don't even make a good junkie.

(*She sits on the wardrobe.*)

EDDIE: (*Shouts*) Tell me where I can get it or I'll kill you.

MAUREEN: No you won't. You haven't got the guts, lover boy. You'd have to look me in the eye to do it. And you've never bothered looking at me once, have you? Have you ever asked how I feel, Mr Fucking Perfect? Do you even know the names of my children?

EDDIE: I don't want to know. I haven't room for your life.

(EDDIE *sits on the wardrobe and* MAUREEN *rises.*)

MAUREEN: I want you to see me, to lift your head and finally acknowledge that I am here. I have lived, I had a family and a house too. First year on the scuttery estate in Balbriggan they had a community week with a bonfire and a monster sing-song. Everybody sitting looking at each other until they started singing the jingles from the ads on television. God, I laughed so much . . . (*her voice drops*) he hit me when we got inside the door. Four years and two kids and I'm only having my twenty-first. We couldn't even have it in the city centre. No, the Grand Hotel on the Main Street, chicken and chips and gawking at the faces from across the road. I drank so much I went walkabout on my way to the ladies, woke up in some fisherman's bed, the middle of the night, the police outside and my husband banging on the door. The fisherman was kneeling up naked, peering out the blinds. I could see how I'd clawed the skin off his back when I came. Four years of my youth to make up in one night. Gerard kept the house and kids, I wasn't thinking much, just wanted time away. He did it all legal like a proper bank clerk, I was signing things I'd only half read. Six months of freedom, I figured, and I'd go back to poxy little Gerard for the kids. Six weeks later I got his postcard with their new address in Canada.

EDDIE: I don't want to hear this, I just want you to give me an address. Where? Do you want me to have to beg you now?

MAUREEN: You listen good. Losing your kids, it's like having the heart torn from you. I was tainted goods at twenty-one. Amazing how men can sense it in a night-club, like they were doing you a big favour letting you suck on their dick. I lost everything to a bastard doing his duty, just looking for an excuse to get away from me. You had a wife and a kid who loved you, you had a home and you just blew it all.

EDDIE: I wanted to know.

MAUREEN: Know what?

EDDIE: How it felt to have the hole in my heart filled. Long ago something was torn out of me, I don't even know what, something that I was one day and wasn't the next. Like a big space rattling around inside me, making me never really belong anywhere, never at ease. Always thought if I had money it would be different, but I don't know. All my life . . .

MAUREEN: (*Quietly*) The corporation gave Eileen a flat. She told me not to tell you the address.

EDDIE: She told my only daughter that I was dead.

MAUREEN: What address do you want, lover boy?

EDDIE: (*Pause*) I want smack to fill me up like sparkling lemonade.

MAUREEN: She told your daughter right. (*Pause.*) The flats below, towards town. The second floor. You can't miss it. They have wooden shutters stuck up on the windows outside since they came up in the world. But it will cost you money, lover boy. You need money now.

EDDIE: No bottle, no warmth.

MAUREEN: What?

EDDIE: A works, I need a works.

MAUREEN: Beside the record player inside, there's a blue vase. Take the syringe that's inside it and may it kill you.

(EDDIE *begins to walk past her.*)

EDDIE: If it has touched your flesh I'm sure it will.

(MAUREEN *exits as* EDDIE *staggers towards the wardrobe and, opening it, begins to root around inside. The* OLD MAN *emerges through the doorway and stands looking at* EDDIE, *lifting his hand to his eyes as if peering through the semi-darkness.*)

OLD MAN: You again, boy? I thought I had taught you a lesson.

(EDDIE *slams the lid of the wardrobe down and climbs up on to it.*)

EDDIE: (*A mumbled, distorted grunt*) Money.

OLD MAN: For what this time? Is your child sick again or is it your pet hamster?

EDDIE: Money, you old bastard, give me money!

OLD MAN: Look at you, boy. You've eyes like those prisoners in the newsreels they showed us after the war.

EDDIE: (*Almost a giggle*) Money, money, money, money.

(*The* OLD MAN *looks at him, his anger gone and a sad authority in his voice.*)

OLD MAN: Go home now, son. For God's sake, before you do yourself harm.

EDDIE: I hate you.

OLD MAN: What have I ever done to you, boy? I don't even know you.

EDDIE: (*Sneering*) 'I built this, I built that.' I hate you. I don't want your money. (*Sudden strength in his voice*) Fuck your money! I want your life. (*He holds his hand out.*) I want to have built things . . . I want to have come home, the good smell of sweat, mortar underneath my nails, dust on my clothes. I want to put money on the table, I want children to look at me with respect. I want . . . I want . . . I want to hold my head up in the supermarket, to walk with a full trolley and not look at the price of things, to see butts on the street and not want to pick them up. I want to have been you, you bastard. (*He pauses, trying to recover his jumbled thoughts.*) I could kill you with envy, I could spit on you the way your eyes spit on me. Come back to life at thirty and I could beat you at anything. Why should the likes of you have had a life and not me?

OLD MAN: I had my poor days too. De Valera's bloody

economic war, recessions, hungry children at the window waiting for me to come in with bread in my pockets. But I never broke into people's houses in the middle of the night. When I fell down I got up again and kept my dignity. Now get the hell out of my house, boy, and stay away from it.

(EDDIE *jumps down from the wardrobe and grabs the man by the shirt. He presses his own face up against his and roars.*)

EDDIE: Give me your life! (*Pause.*) Give me it! Give me! Give!

(*The* OLD MAN *suddenly gasps and raises his own hands to clutch his chest. His throat gives a rattle and* EDDIE *finds he is supporting him. They stagger for a moment, like a drunken couple at a dance, towards the ramp.*)

OLD MAN: The heart, you bastard, my heart.

(*The* OLD MAN *topples back on to the ramp, bringing* EDDIE *to his knees.*)

EDDIE: Don't you fucking die on me. I'm talking to you, I want you to explain . . .

OLD MAN: (*Choked whisper as he tries to call over his shoulder*) Margaret, bolt the door Margaret.

EDDIE: I'm talking to you, I want to talk, do you hear?

OLD MAN: (*Turns head*) A priest, say an act of contrition . . . Oh, my God, I'm heartily sorry for all my sins . . .

EDDIE: (*All the emotion drained from his voice*) . . . because you are so good and with the help of your grace I will never sin again.

(*He grips the man's hand a moment, then rises and slowly backs away. The* HORSE *moves towards him.*)

HORSE: Turn around, Eddie. See the stairs lurching at you as you stumble past him to the bedroom.

EDDIE: (*With his back still to the* HORSE) I don't want to see, I don't . . .

HORSE: See his wife staring from the bed like a shrunken head, bony hands clutching a crucifix. See yourself . . .

EDDIE: I say 'No'.

HORSE: . . . turning the mattress over, no longer even seeing her lying between the bed and the wall, calling 'Larry!

Larry!' The damp feel of those discoloured banknotes. They were for Masses for the dead, Eddie. Robbing the dead.

EDDIE: (*Turns*) No! (*He stops.*) The dead. Save me from them. Following me, chattering inside my head.

HORSE: It's not the dead haunting you. A face in the muck. Not her face, not Brendan, not Orla.

EDDIE: Can't make his features out. Save me from him, save me. Why am I growing so cold, so cold?

HORSE: I have been keeping you warm, running my fingers through your veins, cupping your heart in my palm.
(*The* HORSE *begins to back away from him.*)

EDDIE: Then why are you going away? I've paid my money . . . the things I've done for it. You can't leave me here to face him . . .

HORSE: I'm empty, Eddie, a vast glistening vacuum inside you.
(*He turns to look around in terror, then scrambles towards the syringe on the stage.*)
It's empty, Eddie, nothing left inside but the thinnest of air.

EDDIE: I want you to save me from him, I want . . .
(*He kneels to pick the needle up and as he injects himself his body twists, contorted in pain as the bubble of air reaches his heart. The* HORSE *contorts in pain, echoing his movement. The* OLD MAN *comes to life on the top of the ramp.*)

OLD MAN: Two hours dying on those stairs, boy. All the time I had to curse you, listening to my wife crying in the room upstairs.

EDDIE: Is hell not deep enough for the likes of you?

OLD MAN: Come down and find out son, we're all waiting to bring you with us. On a white horse with the nostrils of Lucifer.
(EDDIE's *body twists again in a painful contortion as the* OLD MAN *speaks. The* HORSE, *who has been watching over him, slowly backs away.*)

OLD MAN: Away with you now boy. Galloping down to hell. Past your brother. How does he look, grinning up after eighteen months in the ground? On down boy, down through the shoals of faces, brushing through their flesh like the webs of spiders, down to the one face that's haunting you. Staring upwards in the winter grass beyond the lights of the caravans.

EDDIE: Who? Who?

OLD MAN: His eyes fixed and cold. His eyes that haunt me, haunt my wife, haunt his father, his wife, his daughter. Face those eyes, boy! Face him!

EDDIE: (*A scream of terror as he falls*) No!

(*As he staggers back the* HORSE *catches him in her arms in the posture of the woman kneeling with the body taken down from the cross.*)

HORSE: You know who it is, Eddie, you are returning back into his body. My power on your limbs is gone. There's just a bubble of air like a diamond in your heart. Feel the muck on your cheek, the icy waters of the Silver Spoon where you used to play, the frost through your clothes. Can anything be colder than that?

EDDIE: My skin.

HORSE: Colder and as stiff to break.

EDDIE: Like my veins were an ice palace for a winter princess. I cannot turn my head. Just a patch of sky, the last few trees on the last headland frozen in my mind. Will I see the face of Christ. I always wanted to know? I had a hole in my heart that now I think nothing else will ever fill, though I spat the wafer out and I'm spitting it out still.

HORSE: Look, Eddie.

EDDIE: Something moving in the trees. White . . . another and another . . . shapes with white manes blowing . . . like they were always there but I could never see them . . . like I was floating up among them through time and sunsets . . . buffeting about in the currents of air . . . hold me . . . hold . . .

HORSE: Look down below you, Eddie. It's dusk again. The green where the ponies are tied, the lights of cars passing. Let yourself fall towards the window on the ground floor of the flats. You are standing unnoticed among the bushes there to gaze in at them. How old the child looks, her mother brushing her hair for bed. The way her grandfather lifts her up when she kisses him. Look, Eddie, see her turning, when she thinks no one is watching, to touch the photograph on the mantelpiece lightly with one finger. Every night the same. And how her mother gazes towards the window until the child runs to take her hand. And out here in the darkness further back behind you, Eddie, if you could only turn your head you would see a woman anxiously watching over you, and behind her another watching over her and another behind her. At every lit window the length of this city a pair of eyes is watching over those who are left inside.

(EDDIE *tries to turn his head but finds that he cannot.*)

EDDIE: What shape have you?

HORSE: A white horse with nostrils flaring. You would know my face if you could only see it.

EDDIE: I need to know. (*Pause. There is a glimpse of joy in his expression.*) Are you my mother?

(*The lights fade.*)

FOR THE BEST IN PAPERBACKS, LOOK FOR THE 🐧

In every corner of the world, on every subject under the sun, Penguin represents quality and variety – the very best in publishing today.

For complete information about books available from Penguin – including Puffins, Penguin Classics and Arkana – and how to order them, write to us at the appropriate address below. Please note that for copyright reasons the selection of books varies from country to country.

In the United Kingdom: Please write to *Dept JC, Penguin Books Ltd, FREEPOST, West Drayton, Middlesex, UB7 0BR.*

If you have any difficulty in obtaining a title, please send your order with the correct money, plus ten per cent for postage and packaging, to *PO Box No 11, West Drayton, Middlesex*

In the United States: Please write to *Dept BA, Penguin, 299 Murray Hill Parkway, East Rutherford, New Jersey 07073*

In Canada: Please write to *Penguin Books Canada Ltd, 2801 John Street, Markham, Ontario L3R 1B4*

In Australia: Please write to the *Marketing Department, Penguin Books Australia Ltd, P.O. Box 257, Ringwood, Victoria 3134*

In New Zealand: Please write to the *Marketing Department, Penguin Books (NZ) Ltd, Private Bag, Takapuna, Auckland 9*

In India: Please write to *Penguin Overseas Ltd, 706 Eros Apartments, 56 Nehru Place, New Delhi, 110019*

In the Netherlands: Please write to *Penguin Books Netherlands B.V., Postbus 3507, NL–1001 AH, Amsterdam*

In West Germany: Please write to *Penguin Books Ltd, Friedrichstrasse 10–12, D–6000 Frankfurt/Main 1*

In Spain: Please write to *Alhambra Longman S.A., Fernandez de la Hoz 9, E–28010 Madrid*

In Italy: Please write to *Penguin Italia s.r.l., Via Como 4, I-20096 Pioltello (Milano)*

In France: Please write to *Penguin France S.A., 17 rue Lejeune, F-31000 Toulouse*

In Japan: Please write to *Longman Penguin Japan Co Ltd, Yamaguchi Building, 2–12–9 Kanda Jimbocho, Chiyoda-Ku, Tokyo 101*

FOR THE BEST IN PAPERBACKS, LOOK FOR THE 🐧

A SELECTION OF FICTION AND NON-FICTION

Cal Bernard Mac Laverty

Springing out of the fear and violence of Ulster, *Cal* is a haunting love story from a land where tenderness and innocence can only flicker briefly in the dark. 'Mac Laverty describes the sad, straitened, passionate lives of his characters with tremendously moving skill' – *Spectator*

The Rebel Angels Robertson Davies

A glittering extravaganza of wit, scatology, saturnalia, mysticism and erudite vaudeville. 'The kind of writer who makes you want to nag your friends until they read him so that they can share the pleasure' – *Observer*

Stars of the New Curfew Ben Okri

'Anarchical energy with authoritative poise … an electrifying collection' – Graham Swift. 'Okri's work is obsessive and compelling, spangled with a sense of exotic magic and haunted by shadows … reality re-dreamt with great conviction' – *Time Out*

The Magic Lantern Ingmar Bergman

'A kaleidoscope of memories intercut as in a film, sharply written and trimmed to the bone' – *Sunday Times*. 'The autobiography is exactly like the films: beautiful and repulsive; truthful and phoney; constantly startling' – *Sunday Telegraph*. 'Unique, reticent, revealing' – Lindsay Anderson

The Horn John Clellon Holmes

Edgar Pool is slave to nothing, not even the genius inside him. He lives no life but jazz, no days but nights wrestling swing out of sordidness in the crowded clubs of New York. And out of obsession with the sound of his tenor sax the legend of bop is born… 'The people … are real, the music is thrilling, and the writing is powerful' – *Chicago Tribune*

The News from Ireland William Trevor

'An ability to enchant as much as chill has made Trevor unquestionably one of our greatest short-story writers' – *The Times*. 'A masterly collection' – *Daily Telegraph*

FOR THE BEST IN PAPERBACKS, LOOK FOR THE

PENGUIN POETRY LIBRARY

Arnold   Selected by Kenneth Allott
Blake   Selected by W. H. Stevenson
Browning   Selected by Daniel Karlin
Burns   Selected by Angus Calder and William Donnelly
Byron   Selected by A. S. B. Glover
Clare   Selected by Geoffrey Summerfield
Coleridge   Selected by Kathleen Raine
Donne   Selected by John Hayward
Dryden   Selected by Douglas Grant
Hardy   Selected by David Wright
Herbert   Selected by W. H. Auden
Keats   Selected by John Barnard
Kipling   Selected by James Cochrane
Lawrence   Selected by Keith Sagar
Milton   Selected by Laurence D. Lerner
Pope   Selected by Douglas Grant
Rubáiyát of Omar Khayyám   Translated by Edward FitzGerald
Shelley   Selected by Isabel Quigley
Tennyson   Selected by W. E. Williams
Wordsworth   Selected by W. E. Williams

FOR THE BEST IN PAPERBACKS, LOOK FOR THE

PENGUIN BOOKS OF POETRY

American Verse
British Poetry Since 1945
Caribbean Verse in English
A Choice of Comic and Curious Verse
Contemporary American Poetry
Contemporary British Poetry
English Christian Verse
English Poetry 1918–60
English Romantic Verse
English Verse
First World War Poetry
Greek Verse
Irish Verse
Light Verse
Love Poetry
The Metaphysical Poets
Modern African Poetry
New Poetry
Poetry of the Thirties
Post-War Russian Poetry
Scottish Verse
Southern African Verse
Spanish Civil War Verse
Spanish Verse
Women Poets

FOR THE BEST IN PAPERBACKS, LOOK FOR THE 🐧

PENGUIN INTERNATIONAL POETS

Anna Akhmatova   Selected Poems   Translated by D. M. Thomas

Anna Akhmatova is not only Russia's finest woman poet but perhaps the finest in the history of western culture.

Fernando Pessoa   Selected Poems

'I have sought for his shade in those Edwardian cafés in Lisbon which he haunted, for he was Lisbon's Cavafy or Verlaine' – Cyril Connolly in the *Sunday Times*

Yehuda Amichai   Selected Poems
Translated by Chana Bloch and Stephen Mitchell

'A truly major poet ... there's a depth, breadth and weighty momentum in these subtle and delicate poems of his' – Ted Hughes

Czeslaw Miłosz   Collected Poems 1931–1987
Winner of the 1980 Nobel Prize for Literature

'One of the greatest poets of our time, perhaps the greatest' – Joseph Brodsky

Joseph Brodsky   To Urania
Winner of the 1987 Nobel Prize for Literature

Exiled from the Soviet Union in 1972, Joseph Brodsky has been universally acclaimed as the most talented Russian poet of his generation.

and

Paul Celan	Selected Poems
Tony Harrison	Selected Poems *and* Theatre Works 1973–1985
Heine	Selected Verse
Geoffrey Hill	Collected Poems
Philippe Jaccottet	Selected Poems
Osip Mandelstam	Selected Poems
Pablo Neruda	Selected Poems
Peter Redgrove	Poems 1954–1987

FOR THE BEST IN PAPERBACKS, LOOK FOR THE 🐧

PLAYS IN PENGUIN

Edward Albee	**Who's Afraid of Virginia Woolf?**
Alan Ayckbourn	**The Norman Conquests**
Bertolt Brecht	**Parables for the Theatre (The Good Woman of Setzuan/The Caucasian Chalk Circle)**
Anton Chekhov	**Plays (The Cherry Orchard/Three Sisters/Ivanov/The Seagull/Uncle Vania)**
Henrik Ibsen	**Hedda Gabler/The Pillars of the Community/The Wild Duck**
Eugène Ionesco	**Rhinoceros/The Chairs/The Lesson**
Ben Jonson	**Three Comedies (Volpone/The Alchemist/Bartholomew Fair)**
D. H. Lawrence	**Three Plays (The Collier's Friday Night/The Daughter-in-Law/The Widowing of Mrs Holroyd)**
Arthur Miller	**Death of a Salesman**
John Mortimer	**A Voyage Round My Father/What Shall We Tell Caroline?/The Dock Brief**
J. B. Priestley	**Time and the Conways/I Have Been Here Before/An Inspector Calls/The Linden Tree**
Peter Shaffer	**Lettice and Lovage/Yonadab**
Bernard Shaw	**Plays Pleasant (Arms and the Man/Candida/The Man of Destiny/You Never Can Tell)**
Sophocles	**Three Theban Plays (Oedipus the King/Antigone/Oedipus at Colonus)**
Arnold Wesker	**Plays, Volume 1: The Wesker Trilogy (Chicken Soup with Barley/Roots/I'm Talking about Jerusalem)**
Oscar Wilde	**The Importance of Being Earnest and Other Plays (Lady Windermere's Fan/A Woman of No Importance/An Ideal Husband/Salome)**
Thornton Wilder	**Our Town/The Skin of Our Teeth/The Matchmaker**
Tennessee Williams	**Cat on a Hot Tin Roof/The Milk Train Doesn't Stop Here Anymore/The Night of the Iguana**

BY THE SAME AUTHOR

The Journey Home

'Hano's initiation into sleazy Dublin nightlife and Shay's fall from grace and eventual tragic humiliation is conveyed with a compelling, even reckless, intensity' – *Irish Independent*

'All 1990s life is there – drink, drugs . . . political corruption, all the words which have been repeated so often now that they have lost their power to shock. Here, they shock' – *Irish Times*

'Joyce, O'Flaherty, Brian Moore, John McGahern, a fistful of O'Brien's. This is a succulent Who's Who of Irish Writing, and Dermot Bolger is of the same ilk . . . an exceptional literary gift' – *Independent*

'Bolger's themes are moral and sexual degradation and the ubiquity of corruption . . . the relentless honesty of his writing is savage and refreshing' – *Time Out*

'Within two pages you want to know desperately what happens to his characters . . . the most remarkable novel to come out of Ireland that I have read in the last fifteen or twenty years' – Frank Delaney on *First Edition*, RTE